Protestant Worship and
Church Architecture

Protestant Worship and Church Architecture

THEOLOGICAL AND HISTORICAL CONSIDERATIONS

JAMES F. WHITE

Perkins School of Theology
Southern Methodist University
Dallas, Texas

Wipf and Stock Publishers
EUGENE, OREGON

Wipf and Stock Publishers
199 West 8th Avenue, Suite 3
Eugene, Oregon 97401

Protestant Worship and Church Architecture
Theological and Historical Considerations
By White, James F.
Copyright© January, 1964 White, James F.
ISBN: 1-59244-163-7
Publication date: February, 2003
Previously published by Oxford University Press, January, 1964 .

To my parents:
E. Turner White
Madeline R. White
who have visited countless churches with me

Preface

Each year a billion dollars are spent on church buildings in this country. Yet, there is no book available to guide building committees, ministers, and others responsible for new churches in the theological and historical implications of their work. This is not only a paradox; it is a tragedy. To spend so much time and so much money without an understanding of the basic principles involved is an extraordinary misfortune. Worse than that, it often means that the buildings are detrimental to the life and mission of the Church instead of being beneficial. Increasingly we realize the relevance of the Christian message for all aspects of our daily life. Surely we cannot afford to ignore the importance of theology in building a church. Neither can we afford to be ignorant of the traditions which we as the Church represent.

The opportunity to build a new church occurs only once or twice in each generation of church members. It is all the more important that it be done carefully since the building will continue to affect the life of the congregation, "for better for worse," ever after. This can be a great opportunity for any congregation. The experience of erecting a new building has been a time of renewal in the life of many congregations. St. Thomas Aquinas once wrote that "the house [of God] signifies the Church," meaning that the building makes known or denotes what the Church is. Frequently while building, congregations have realized what it means to be the Church. More than one congregation has first come to know what the Church really signifies during the process of planning for a new house of God. Certainly one of the most important occasions for discovering what the Church does in worship and the rest of its life together comes while providing shelter for these activities.

This book is intended for building committees and others concerned with the problems of building for Christian worship. It is meant to help in exploring some of the basic theological and historical concerns that must be discussed before any satisfactory church building can be erected. Until the fundamental questions as to what the Church is and what the Church does in worship are raised, a congregation is not prepared to build. These, of course, are theological questions and it is hoped that this book will be of help to laymen in this area. But we do not build in a historical vacuum. Each congregation is part of a tradition and needs to know what made it that which it now is before it can understand itself. Accordingly, I have included a historical survey to help congregations in this exercise of self-understanding. I believe it should also indicate the tremendous variety of possibilities open to us, many of which have been ignored too long. This book tries to point to the most significant theological and historical concerns present in providing an architectural setting for Protestant worship.

The revolution going on in architecture is paralleled in many ways by the theological turmoil of our times. Many ministers find that theological scholarship and discussion have moved away from positions which were familiar to them as seminary students. This book and the articles and books cited herein should help them remain current in contemporary thought about worship. Some of the historical evidence is assembled here for the first time but it should be obvious that there remains much further research to be done in every tradition if we are to profit fully from the experiences of the past.

I have tried to limit my material to that which would be of direct interest to all the major Protestant bodies in this country.

This has not always been easy since even the words used change from one denomination to another. For a Baptist a baptistery can mean something quite different from what it signifies to a Roman Catholic. Sanctuary means one thing to a Methodist, another to an Episcopalian. I have tried to use language which would be clear to most American Protestants even though this has often meant avoiding the technical language of the architectural historian or theologian.

This book is concerned only with the portion of the church building used for worship. I have used the word "church" in this sense. It is quite true that in America the space used for worship may be a relatively small portion of the total building but, if the thesis of this book be correct, it is by far the most important part. Other books, particularly those issued by denominational building agencies, give details on building for educational, recreational, and social activities. There are also a number of books available on means of raising funds, dealings with the architect, and terms of a contract. Some of these are listed in the bibliography. I have consciously avoided duplicating this material since it is readily accessible.

I would like to thank Mr. Decherd H. Turner for his constant help in securing books and for his frequent encouragement. His associates at Bridwell Library, Mrs. Elizabeth Twitchell and Mrs. John H. Warnick, have been most gracious in their assistance. I wish to thank the Reverend Wilfred M. Bailey and Mr. Downing A. Thomas, A.I.A., for reading the manuscript and making many perceptive comments. Lastly, my thanks go to my wife, Marilyn, for typing, proofreading, and most of all for putting up with me when I was thinking about the book and without me while I was writing it.

Dallas, Texas   J. F. W.
May 1964

Contents

Protestant Worship and
Church Architecture

I

Two Approaches to Worship

Protestants today seem to approach public worship with one or the other of two quite different attitudes. Many Protestants understand worship as primarily a matter of feelings; others see worship as basically work done in God's service. To be sure, most people are hardly aware of the conceptions with which they approach worship. Far from being deliberate principles, these attitudes are rarely examined.

Before we begin to discuss Protestant church building it is necessary to analyze the ideas about public worship which prevail in our time. The two prevalent attitudes—worship as centered in the feelings and worship as work done—will be examined in this chapter.

I

It is very common to hear people speak of "getting something" out of worship. Behind such a phrase lies a number of assumptions, particularly the concept that one receives "something" out of worship. Strangely enough, the nature of this "something" is not very clear. Each year the advertising media urge us to worship in the church of our choice. Sometimes we are told that it will enhance our family life; at other times we are advised that we will be better persons for having worshiped.

If one examines these reasons for advocating worship they seem to have one common basis, namely that worship does *something for us*. Worship, we assume, must have some effect upon us.

More and more it seems that the effects sought in worship are primarily concerned with the emotions or feelings. When we speak of "getting something" out of worship we usually refer to receiving some kind of feeling as a result of having worshiped. The emotions involved cover a tremendous range. Some denominations, to be sure, cultivate emotional excitement to a much greater extent than others, but this effort to produce a sense of adjustment with the universe, or contrition for one's sin, or some other type of feeling is not limited by any denominational barriers.

Our emotional responses become, to a large extent, our means of judging what we call the "worship experience." On this basis services are judged and even criticized as being successful or unsuccessful. The most negative remark about a service is that it "leaves me cold," which is to say that it fails to elicit any emotional response. On the other hand, we occasionally hear services of worship praised for giving one "a good feeling."

Surprisingly enough, the feelings that people seek from worship are hard to define precisely. The more one discusses the type of service from which people claim to "get something," the more varied the types appear to be. One sees people enthusiastic over the feeling of exultation some services and occasions elicit. Others seem to seek from worship a feeling of security, a Browning-like assurance ("God's in His heaven—All's right with the world!"). There are others for whom worship is an opportunity to experience a deep sense of sorrow for their sinfulness. Indeed, almost the whole gamut of emotions seems to be found in worship at one time or another.

One is led to conclude that the personality of the individual has much to do with the particular type of emotion most commonly associated with worship. But even more important than the type of emotion sought seems to be the intensity of it. A service of worship is criticized more for producing no feeling than it is for producing a defective kind. Emotional neutrality seems to many people to be a flaw in worship perhaps even worse than the wrong type of emotional appeal.

Precisely because of this concern with worship as a matter of feeling, great care has been shown by those responsible for planning and conducting services of worship that the worshipers might not be disappointed. Whether we like to admit it or not, ministers have long been accustomed to making provision for the emotional content of services. Much of the literature on church architecture devotes considerable attention to this approach to worship. Indeed, stimulating the desired emotional responses has become something of a science.

The chief means of manipulating the emotional content of a service of worship is through the appeal of the senses. Usually this is done in a subtle fashion by atmosphere. The term "worshipful atmosphere" appears constantly in recent discussions of church architecture. We will leave till later our discussion of a "worshipful atmosphere" in church architecture, but let us see what this term means for other art forms.

We have become quite accustomed now to think of music as background atmosphere for all types of institutions, from supermarkets to funeral parlors. Before movies had sound tracks, pianists or organists were often employed to accompany the action on the screen. Music was a background for what the eye saw, but it was more than this, for it added to the emotional intensity of exciting scenes or reflected the calm of placid episodes. In many churches music is used to fulfill a similar function. Congregations grow accustomed to lolling in musical enrichments, particularly deep pedal stops on the organ during prayers. At times choirs are used for a similar effect; emotional conditioning of the congregation becomes one of their responsibilities.

Music has tremendous powers to manipulate the emotions of

the hearers as well as those of the performers. So great were these powers that Plato was wary of exposing the youth to types of music which might excite the wrong emotions.[1] Possibly it is a perversion of music to use it to condition others, but it seems to be deliberately used for this purpose in some services of worship.

The other arts, particularly painting, stained glass, and sculpture have often been used to produce an emotional climate. This is especially obvious in rococo churches with their swirling saints and festoons of lavish carvings. But even in less elegant buildings the arts are frequently employed, using the sense of sight to elicit feelings associated with worship.

The effort to create a worshipful atmosphere, then, depends primarily upon conditioning the senses of sight and hearing to produce a favorable emotional response. Our churches make little appeal to the senses of smell, touch, or taste, though ample care is often taken to secure adequate ventilation and comfortable seating so that there will be no interference with the appeals to the other senses.

The emotional response solicited in these instances is a passive and individualistic matter. The congregation does nothing to create the worshipful atmosphere of the building and it may do little to produce the music. The emphasis, instead, is upon the congregation's receiving, individual by individual, that which is provided by others. Thus worship, conceived of as a matter of feeling, often becomes a private and passive reception of the emotive factors of the service.

When one looks at the historical background for the modern concentration upon worship as a matter of feeling it seems surprisingly recent in origin. Although one may detect strains of this approach in the German Pietism of the late seventeenth century, and in Methodism and the Great Awakening in the eighteenth century, it was not until the nineteenth century that the feelings

---

[1] *The Republic*, III, 398.

of the worshiper really became the prime focus in worship. It came most conspicuously as a consequence of the revival system but even those who differed most widely from the revivalists were affected by it.

The practice of conducting revivals of religion began in the eighteenth century, but revivalism became perfected into a system in nineteenth-century America. During the nineteenth century revivalism succeeded in Christianizing this country, turning a semi-pagan population into a people predominantly Christian.[2] One cannot question the tremendous influence which revivalism has had on shaping every aspect of American Protestantism, particularly worship.

One of the most important aspects of revivalism was a strong insistence upon the necessity of a conscious conversion experience. Revivalism could almost be said to exist for the purpose of producing a conversion experience in which the sinner was gloriously transformed. The most characteristic sign of this change was an emotional crisis in which one's past existence was cast aside for a renewed life. "Getting religion" was characterized by going through a definite experience involving an emotional crisis. The same concepts of conversion persist in this century. Professor George A. Coe wrote of an individual who "sought in vain for twelve years to attain what he was taught to expect; another sought for eight years, another for four or five."[3] The desired emotional experience is all-important to many people since they feel no genuine Christian life is possible without it.

Protestant Christianity was most adept at producing the means for conversion experiences. Indeed, the means were developed into a system. Many aspects of the revival system originated on

[2] Franklin Littell, *From State Church to Pluralism; A Protestant Interpretation of Religion in American History* (New York: Doubleday, 1962), pp. 46–62.

[3] *The Spiritual Life; Studies in the Science of Religion* (New York: Eaton and Mains, 1900), p. 150.

the frontier in camp meetings where settlers assembled at certain occasions for periods of worship. Peter Cartwright, the famous Methodist circuit rider, testified that "many happy thousands were awakened and converted to God at these camp meetings . . . until our country seemed all coming home to God." [4] In the 1830s revivalism penetrated the churches on the east coast though not without stubborn resistance. Charles G. Finney, who symbolized the revival system, brought his "new measures" to New York City. One can see in his published *Lectures on Revivals of Religion* (1835) a determination to use whatever means were available to bring the unrepentant to God through a conversion experience. Finney scorned traditional forms of worship unless they were efficacious in producing conversions.[5]

Revivalism had some great consequences for Protestant worship. It tended to concentrate on the individual, since its purpose was conversion of the individual. But since the individual was often reached through the emotional fervor of the entire congregation, methods were developed to heighten the emotional intensity of the group, converted and unconverted. A specific type of church music was produced, the gospel song. Generally the gospel songs recounted the emotional experiences of those already converted but they also were used to make such experiences attractive to the unconverted. Worship tended to revolve around the reliving of these experiences on the part of the converted and inducing the unconverted to have similar experiences.

Such practices had a most significant effect on Protestant worship, for they made worship largely a means to an end, the end being conversion. Thus in worship one hoped for the emotional climax in which he passed from the number of the damned to the company of the saved. Having passed this decisive event, worship

[4] *Autobiography* (New York: Methodist Book Concern, 1856), p. 46.

[5] *Lectures on Revivals of Religion,* edited by William G. McLoughlin (Cambridge, Mass.: Harvard University Press, 1960), Ch. 14.

remained a recalling of the crucial moment in order to live one's life in the radiancy of the grace that made conversion possible. The concern was always for the feelings induced by worship. Dozens of books were written on how to conduct revivals with careful attention to means and measures of producing the appropriate feelings.

Early in the twentieth century there developed a keen interest among scholars in the psychology of conversion. Their work reveals a confidence that they could use scientific methods in studying the religious consciousness. Professor Coe stated the program of many of these men:

The religious processes taking place around us and within us must be observed with all the precision that modern psychological methods and tools render possible. For, whatever else religion may or may not be, it is at least a mass of ascertainable states of consciousness; and in the absence of information to the contrary we must presume that such states can be analyzed and described, and that their relations to one another and to the recognized laws of the mental and bodily life can be to some extent determined. What is needed is an examination of the facts as such, without reference to their possible bearing upon theology or philosophy.[6]

Although most of these writers found revivalism distasteful, they remained fascinated by the states of mind connected with conversion. Though they analyzed the psychological processes of conversion with scientific detachment, many of these scholars were also interested in a constructive application of their findings to the role of emotions in the Christian life.

The results of the psychological studies of religious experience were especially fascinating to those scholars doing the most advanced thinking in religious education early in this century. Many of these men had a great interest in worship. Whereas most books written on worship in the last two decades would probably be found to come from the pens of theologians and his-

[6] Coe, *The Spiritual Life* . . . , p. 5.

torians, the first decades of this century found people whose training was in religious education producing many of the important books on the subject.

Many of these writers considered worship primarily as a matter of emotional experience or "religious experience," as they preferred to call it. The liberal theological currents of the day stressed the desirability of such experiences. Professor Henry Nelson Wieman wrote:

In the collective worship conducted by a crowd *the chief end is to produce the emotional glow and satisfaction that comes from feeling that we are all together and having the same experience.* Each member of the crowd is brought to a state of acute suggestibility by the interacting of many individuals on one another so that any thought or feeling suggested by the leader is transmitted to every one in the crowd and is tremendously intensified by the stimulus of many people interacting on one another in having the same experience.[7]

Here we see a sophisticated theologian interpreting one kind of worship having as its "end" the production of certain feelings, yet any backwoods revivalist might speak in very similar terms. One finds similar sentiments in many others concerned with religious education at that time. Marie Cole Powell wrote in 1935, "As we pause to think of some . . . great moment of worship, we probably realize that in that moment something vital happened to us. In other words, worship is first of all an experience."[8] It is significant that the title of her book is *Guiding the Experience of Worship*, written not long after Professor Edwin H. Byington's *The Quest for Experience in Worship*.

Such experiences as these people sought to produce seem to be

[7] *Methods of Private Religious Living* (New York: Macmillan, 1929), pp. 116–17 (italics added).

[8] *Guiding the Experience of Worship* (New York: Abingdon-Cokesbury, 1935), p. 14. Edwin H. Byington called worship "a satisfying and rewarding experience," *The Quest for Experience in Worship* (New York: Doubleday, Doran, and Co., 1929), p. 157.

largely a matter of emotions. Indeed the very term "worship experience" has come to be synonymous with a time of emotional intensity. In this there is a real parallel to the concentration on feeling in revivalist worship though the types of emotions may be quite different. Both religious educators and revivalists saw worship as primarily individualistic and subjective. Both agreed the presence of others was not essential to either worship experience or conversion experience. All that matters is that something happens to the individual.

Many of the writers of the time found worship helpful in promoting certain goals, especially social reforms. Miss Powell found worship producing a desire for higher values by an "emotional glow which renews the worshiper's hope of ethical and spiritual achievement." [9] No more eloquent advocate of this appeared than Charles Clayton Morrison, editor of the *Christian Century*, who felt that worship should arouse men to join in the social crusades of their day.[10] Professor Wieman found one of the purposes of worship to be the provision of "a readjustment of personal attitude to the end of living more successfully." [11] Most writers agreed that beautiful surroundings were important, if not essential, in producing the desired experience. The psychological information gained by scholars was utilized to make these experiences more readily achieved.

Such tendencies were not without critics. In 1925 Dean Willard Sperry of Harvard addressed a rebuke to the writers of current manuals on worship:

Frank resort to devices suggested by modern psychology, whether of the unconscious or of the herd, does not make for moral confidence in a service of worship which is supposedly addressed to God. They

[9] *Guiding the Experience of Worship*, p. 16.

[10] *The Social Gospel and the Christian Cultus* (New York: Harper and Brothers, 1933).

[11] *Methods of Private Religious Living*, p. 120.

suggest a back-stage apparatus for the manipulation of souls which is too mechanical. . . . The elder theology was on morally safer ground when it held that grace is the gift and work of God.[12]

Others also condemned the manipulative tendencies of the students of psychology and their tendency to exploit the feelings of worshipers for various causes, no matter how good these causes were in themselves.

Still it seems likely that the approach to worship as primarily a matter of feeling is that most widely held among American Protestants today. This attitude seems to be such a basic part of our assumptions about worship that most American Protestants probably are not even aware of an alternative approach.

II

When worship is viewed primarily as the imparting of certain feelings to the worshiper the emphasis is upon the experience of the individual, who may remain quite passive. Worship considered primarily as work done in God's service has a radically different focus. Here the feelings of the individual are secondary. The concentration is upon something that is done. Various acts are performed, such as kneeling, singing, making an offering, and these are done not to condition the worshiper, but as work done, for one reason or another, in God's service. The doing of these things is work. Even though they are not arduous they are performed as work in which each member of the congregation has his particular tasks to fulfill.

It can be seen in this sense that worship necessarily becomes an active thing. The congregation cannot remain passive. Neither can such worship be considered primarily an emotional experience. It becomes instead an act of giving of one's time and work.

---

[12] Willard L. Sperry, *Reality in Worship: A Study of Public Worship and Private Religion* (New York: Macmillan, 1925), p. 170.

This is not to deny that something is received in worship when it is regarded as work. However, the emphasis on giving is directed away from the giver (man) to the recipient (God). Such an attitude is concerned more about the performance of worship than about its effects.

It will be helpful to explore very briefly the significance of work in Christianity, particularly as it is expressed in the Bible. The contemporary notion of work as a laborious necessity, a necessary evil, is far from the understanding of work expressed in the Bible. Not only does the Bible view work as a normal part of life but it also becomes the means by which man serves God. Psalm 104 speaks of the coherent functioning of God's universe in which "Man goes forth to his work and to his labor until evening" as naturally as the sun rises and sets. The fourth commandment states in positive terms: "Six days you shall labor, and do all your work." Work then seems to be a natural and normal part of creation.[13] The soil was cursed in the account of man's fall but not the toil of man who had been placed in the Garden "to till it and keep it."

Work has additional significance since the Hebrew viewed God as One Who works. Psalm 104 is an eloquent praise of God for His works which create nature and provide for His creatures: "These all look to thee, to give them their food in due season." The psalmist praises God, "O Lord, how manifold are thy works!" and sees God as rejoicing in His works. The concepts of God's works and acts on behalf of His people run through both Old and New Testaments. For the Christian this is seen supremely in God's acting through the person of Jesus in the time of the first century.

Man is placed in the world not simply as an autonomous worker in an indifferent universe but in a place where he acts as a servant of God. The Old Testament is particularly fond of re-

[13] Alan Richardson, *The Biblical Doctrine of Work* (London: S.C.M., 1952), pp. 25-9.

ferring to God's people as God's servants. "Ye servants of God, your Master proclaim," wrote Charles Wesley, echoing the language of the Old Testament. The character of a servant, of course, is that of someone who works for someone else. One serves God through one's treatment of his fellow servants, especially in labor which is beneficial to them.

The line between the work of worship and the work of earning a livelihood is a very fine distinction since both are part of man's proper service to God. The manner in which one treats his neighbor is directly a part of his relationship to God. A New Testament passage indicates, "As you did it to one of the least of these my brethren, you did it to me" (Matt. 25:40). Work as service of God is by no means limited to the work of worship. In the New Testament the same word is used for worship, acts of charity, and the work of the pagan civil authorities. All this work serves God in performing a beneficial service for mankind. Luther captured the same idea when he stated that all Christians are priests to each other, "and every one by means of his own work or office must benefit and serve every other." [14] Each member of society performs services that are beneficial to the community and in so doing serves God.

There are several reasons why the special work of worship is necessary. In the first place there is an inevitability about worship as man worships spontaneously out of joy and gladness. "To have a God," said Luther, "is simply to trust and believe in one with our whole heart." [15] It seems only natural that a life changed by such trust and belief should focus its response to God in acts of worship. The work of worship then becomes a spontaneous reaction of joy as suggested in Psalm 98, "O sing to the Lord a

[14] "An Open Letter to the Christian Nobility of the German Nation," *Works of Martin Luther* (Philadelphia ed.; Philadelphia: Muhlenberg, 1943), II, p. 69.

[15] *Dr. Martin Luther's Large Catechism* (Minneapolis: Augsburg, 1935), p. 44.

new song, for he has done marvelous things!" Worship becomes
an acknowledgment of God's love in which man shows his trust
in Him Who first loved man. In this manner worship has as its
purpose the glorification of God Who is its recipient. Indeed, to
glorify God may well be interpreted as one of the chief ends of
man's life.

In another way, the work of worship is done as obedience.
There is a sense in which love obligates us to respond with action,
a sense known to every husband who voluntarily washes dishes.
Yet worship never becomes a good work that obligates God to
reward us, any more than one can bargain for love. God's love
always precedes our response.

In the Old Testament the covenantal relationship reflected the
belief that to be God's possession His people were called to be "a
kingdom of priests and a holy nation," an idea reflected in the
New Testament as "a royal priesthood, a holy nation." The worst
deed God's people could do was to worship other gods besides
the "Lord your God." Such acts so polluted their relationship
with God that the covenant was broken. Those who disobeyed
by worshiping other gods were rejected. Hosea represented God
as calling them, "Not my people, for you are not my people and
I am not your God." The only Old Testament alternative to the
worship of God was idolatry, the worship of false gods, not
atheism, the service of none. Worship then was a part of the life
of God's servant, a work based upon obligation though the work
might be most joyful. Thus a child sometimes does the will of
his parent with pleasure though it still remains an act of obedience.

Worship as obedience is not tied to the performance of any
special form of worship. It is the imperative to do worship that
is fundamental not the prescription of its forms. The communion
services of several denominations include the phrase that it is "our
bounden duty, that we should at all times, and in all places, give
thanks." In this sense of a "bounden duty," worship becomes an

act of obedience performed as a part of man's proper service to God. Worship, then, can be seen as something done simply as a duty to God rather than carried out to accomplish some purpose.

There is another manner in which worship appears as a matter of work. This is in connection with the concept of sacrifice. Actually sacrifice in the Old Testament (and New) involves an immense variety of ideas. We can only touch briefly on a few of these. In one fashion sacrifice is a giving of ourselves through something that we do or have produced. We refer to our worship as a "sacrifice of praise and thanksgiving," for in performing these acts we are offering our work. What is given, however, is a token of the total life and work of the giver. And it is not lost but received back with the power of God, much as the bread and wine in holy communion, which are offered to God, are blessed, broken, and then given back to God's people conveying new power. What has been given, our work of worship as a part of our life surrendered, is given back as new life achieved.[16]

Another concept of sacrifice seems to be of particular interest to Christians. This is the idea that in our work of worship, in offering "our sacrifice of praise and thanksgiving," we are united to Christ's sacrifice for our behalf on the cross. St. Augustine points out that in what the Church offers (her worship), "she herself is offered in the very offering she makes to God." [17] These concepts are particularly germane to the holy communion. A modern French Protestant speaks of this sacrament as "the *offering* which the Church makes of itself to the Father, united to the Son's intercession." [18] What is offered is our own work of wor-

[16] Evelyn Underhill, *Worship* (London: Nisbet and Co., 1937), pp. 57-9.

[17] *City of God*, X, 6, translated by Gerald Walsh and Grace Monahan (New York: Fathers of the Church, Inc., 1952), p. 127.

[18] Max Thurian, *The Eucharistic Memorial; Part II—The New Testament*, translated by J. G. Davies (London: Lutterworth, 1961), p. 76.

ship, but through this we are united to Christ's eternal work on our behalf.

Worship, then becomes work performed as a natural response, as obedience, and as an offering. When worship is viewed primarily as work done in God's service it has a profound consequence for all of man's work. In worship a bit of our work is offered to God, making it easier for us to realize that in actuality all of our work is performed as service to Him. A part of our work thus represents the whole of it. This means that whatever we do to our fellow man immediately affects our relationship to the divine. It also indicates that worship gives meaning to our daily work in helping us to see it, too, as an offering to God. Nothing in life is theologically neutral. The priesthood of all believers is realized in one's occupation, whatever it may be; but it is in performing the special work of worship that this becomes clear to us. It is perhaps not entirely by chance that business firms now prefer to refer to themselves as "services." We see firms advertised as roofing services, typing services, or repair services. Exactly the same term is used for worship when we speak of the "morning service" or the "evening service." In a real sense both are one, for work done in the service of the community or work done in worship are both means of serving God. Worship has profound implications for social responsibility but certainly not by imploring or threatening people to reform their behavior. It goes deeper than this; worship gives meaning to all our work so that it can be judged in its true light as service of God.

The tradition of approaching worship as an act of work, as has been indicated, is already present in the Bible. Indeed the word used in the New Testament for public work is also used for worship (Acts 13:2). Something of the same idea was preserved in the Church, particularly in the term used for the daily services that the monastic orders performed. These services became known as offices, a term derived from *officium* (duty, service).

Saying the daily offices was doing the work of worship and this was often referred to as *opus Dei*, the work of God.

Protestants have long regarded worship primarily as work done. The Catechism of the 1662 *Book of Common Prayer* lists as a part of man's "duty towards God" the need "to worship him," and the 1928 American version contains the statement, "My bounden duty is to follow Christ, to worship God every Sunday in his Church; and to work and pray and give for the spread of his kingdom." Among Presbyterians the Westminster Confession of Faith (1647) likewise laid down the Christian man's obligation to devote time every Sunday to "public and private exercises of his [God's] worship." It is only in comparatively recent times that Protestants have come to look upon worship as primarily concerned with the feelings instead of being a matter of work done in God's service.

III

In the course of history some dangers in approaching worship primarily as a matter of work have become apparent. The work of worship is not intended as a good work that will obligate God to benefit the worshiper. One does not serve God in order to serve oneself. Most Protestants insist that man is justified through a relationship of faith with God and that work becomes a natural response of gratitude to God. But, when good deeds are perverted into a means of trying to merit salvation, Protestants protest. Worship is not intended to produce righteousness but to thank God for imputing His righteousness to us. It cannot be stressed too strongly that men are justified through faith, not by works.

There is also a danger in identifying any particular form of worship as that prescribed by God. Over the centuries the forms of Christian worship have shown considerable variety.

If there are dangers in worship's being considered as work

done in God's service, there are even greater dangers in worship's being approached as a matter of feeling. The most obvious problem is that this orients worship toward man instead of pointing to God. When this happens worship runs a real danger of becoming egocentric, something to please or even entertain the worshipers. Worship performed for such a purpose is directed to an end that is not sufficient. The basic difficulty with such an approach is that its purpose is a selfish one, a narrowly utilitarian performance in order that the worshipers may be satisfied.

But there is a less obvious danger in worship centered upon man's feelings; the fullness of Christian worship is likely to become obscured by such an attitude. To make worship largely dependent upon transient moods is to concentrate upon only one aspect of worship and to sacrifice the most important aspects. It is tragic how many dimensions of worship have been lost to our consciousness in the last hundred years. Many denominations have, in effect, sold their birthright in worship for a pot of porridge.

Far more is involved in worship than simply our feelings about God and man. In worship our relationships to God and man are constituted so that our whole *being* is changed. This is not simply a temporary emotional spree but an enduring transformation of our beliefs, our activities, and indeed our relationship to being in general. Writing on the religious affections in the eighteenth century, Jonathan Edwards pointed out that feelings were transient and could not be adequate gauges of a person's relationship to God.[19] Worship changes one's being by uniting him to a community of faith. As such, he is placed in a new relationship to God, to his fellow Christian, and to the world. But this new being is not something effected by man's efforts or gauged by his sincerity. He comes into his fullness by being made a member of the community united to God in faith. And this community, the

[19] *Religious Affections*, edited by John E. Smith (New Haven: Yale University Press, 1959).

Church, is established not by the efforts of man but by the grace of Christ.

It is important to remember that Christ is present in, with, and through the acts that we perform in worship. According to His will, His work is accomplished through what we do when we gather for worship. The work of worship that we offer can be a means of receiving Christ. Through His grace, the acts that we perform in celebrating holy communion become a means for the building up of His Church. Preaching and listening to preaching are acts of man through which God's Word addresses men. It is indeed misleading to distinguish in worship between acting and receiving for both occur simultaneously. Our giving is receiving. Christ may work in the worship we offer.

The unique quality of Christian worship is that it centers upon the work of God in Christ in establishing a community of those who are enabled to worship Him. It is by the power of God that men are united in receiving what God has done for them. The Pauline metaphor, the "body of Christ," expresses most concisely the nature of the Church. Just as no part of the human body can exist independently of the rest, so Christians cannot exist without the Church. John Calvin was merely echoing a third-century theologian when he observed that he saw no "hope for any forgiveness of sins or any salvation" outside of the Church.[20] Christian worship, then, is the worship of those who "are one body in Christ, and individually members one of another."

In this sense we refer to Christian worship as corporate worship, that is, the worship of those who are one body, the body of Christ. This important fact distinguishes Christian worship from all other worship offered in this world. It has a unity which the dimensions of time and space cannot overcome.

This corporateness in Christ is expressed in Christian worship

[20] *Calvin: Institutes of the Christian Religion*, IV, i, 4, translated by Ford L. Battles and edited by John T. McNeill (Philadelphia: Westminster, 1960), II, 1016.

by two distinct disciplines, personal devotions and common worship. It should be made very clear that personal devotions and common worship are both corporate in nature. In personal devotions one does not approach God as the "alone with the Alone," but as a member of the body of Christ even though the other members are not physically present. Likewise it should be remembered that personal devotions and common worship have always been regarded as complementing and depending upon each other. Neither discipline is superior to the other; both suffer when one is neglected. They do, however, have some quite different characteristics aside from the corporate nature that unites them.

The most obvious condition of personal devotions is that the individual does not depend upon the presence of other worshipers. He may be in their midst in church; he may be at the ends of the earth. It is quite possible to be among those engaged in common worship yet to be resolutely pursuing personal devotions at the same time, as in the cases of a Protestant's engaging in his own prayers during an anthem or a Roman Catholic's saying his rosary during mass.

Since one does not need verbal communication, personal devotions are not necessarily expressed in words. The emotions are very definitely a part of personal devotions. Such devotions often are simply an inarticulate sense of awe in the midst of the beauties of art or nature. Feelings of gratitude or dependence upon God are commonly a part of personal devotions. Church music and architecture have sought very successfully to promote personal devotions.

The emotional latitude in this type of worship is almost unlimited. It can vary from the heights of ecstatic rapture to the depths of self-accusing contrition. The personality of each individual plays a large part in determining the emotional tone of personal devotions since the situation of each individual is paramount here.

On the other hand it would be wrong to assert that the feelings are the chief components of personal devotions. Many Christians know the deficiencies of a devotional life in which they have relied almost exclusively on emotions. The experience of Christendom has been that personal devotions, though free, do require a discipline in order to fulfill themselves. A set pattern of daily devotions is generally acknowledged to be vital. Bible reading has always been a vital part of personal devotions. Other books have often been regarded as of great value too. Meditation is especially important even though what is apparently a simple procedure turns out upon examination to require a careful discipline.

The discipline of common worship is different in several ways from that of personal devotions. Probably most writers today would agree that the statement quoted earlier from Professor Wieman is misleading. Common worship is much more than the personal devotions of individuals being magnified by being conducted in a crowd. No term describes common worship better than the traditional term, which has almost disappeared from the Protestant's vocabulary, the word liturgy. It is quite wrong to think of liturgy as restricted to ceremony with complicated "smells and bells" and all the externals of a Roman Catholic high mass. The word liturgy derives from a Greek term, *leitourgia*, a term referring to the performance of a public task expected of citizens of ancient Athens. It simply meant fulfilling the civil obligations. A true Athenian did this work, not foreigners or slaves. The origin of the term lies in the Greek word *laos* meaning people and the term *ergon* meaning work. It meant the work of the people, and the Christian Church retained this concept in applying the word to common worship. A Christian was one who did his *leitourgia* with the Church. Quite possibly the term used for the Church (*ecclesia*) was limited at first to the assembly that met to perform its work of worship. Liturgy, for the

Christian, is the performance of the work of worship in his new citizenship as one of the people of God.

Basically the word liturgy is most congenial to Protestants, even though unused. It implies that all the people of God are expected to perform their proper work (as were all Athenian citizens). For the Christian this is especially by public worship. In the liturgical assembly the work of Christ is continued, as all Christians share in the high-priestly nature of their Saviour by being priests to their fellow man. One can speak of the liturgy as an extension of the historic incarnation. Christ is embodied in those united in doing their liturgy. In this work the worshipers partake of the whole of Christ through sharing in the portion of His body manifest in each worshiping congregation.[21] The worshiper transcends his individuality in common worship as he is made a part of the whole body of Christ. A new reality is created in the oneness given in common worship.

For common worship to be possible a very definite discipline is necessary. Three factors seem to be vital for common worship. An agreement in the structure of the service, in the words used, and in the actions employed seems to be essential. Without these conventions it is difficult, if not impossible, for all to participate fully.

Obviously a service would soon degenerate into chaos if everyone did something different at the same time. Many groups have drawn up books or orders of worship to make the same structure available to the entire congregation. Likewise common worship depends upon the use of the same words. We cannot say a prayer or creed altogether unless we use the same words. Christian worship is largely dependent upon words, though in some religions other means, such as dancing, may predominate. The third essential for common worship is agreement upon actions. We act to-

[21] Cf. W. Stählin, " 'Koinonia' and Worship," *Studia Liturgica*, I (1962), pp. 220–27.

gether to praise God, confess sin, and attend to the reading and expounding of God's Word.

Unlike personal devotions, common worship can be participated in and shared by all present. It does not require any particular emotions. Feelings are present, of course, for otherwise we would be less than human. But in common worship the emotions are disciplined by the use of the same structure, identical words, and similar actions. Common worship is work in which all can engage, not just those attuned to a certain emotional pitch.

Nothing that has been said has been intended to disparage the importance of personal devotions with their large mixture of feelings. But it should be clear that personal devotions are only a part of the totality of Christian worship, and perhaps a bit less important than common worship where the life in the body of Christ is fully constituted. Personal devotions add to the fullness of common worship and common worship in turn gives scope to personal devotions. It would be misguided effort to try to have one without the other.

There is great peril in approaching worship primarily as a matter of feeling, for this is to limit it almost entirely to the conditions of personal devotions. Within such circumscribed limits the full meaning of common worship is never discovered. We must go beyond feeling in our public worship and see it as work done in common. It is only when worship is understood as work done in God's service as common worship that it reaches its real depth.

Personal devotions with their attendant emotions are of great importance. On the other hand, even more important is the Church's offering of its common worship, its liturgy as work done in God's service. In this sense we can speak of liturgical architecture in referring to the buildings designed to be the place where the work of common worship takes place in space and time. This is not to say that such buildings are unfit for personal devotions, but simply that the chief purpose of these structures is to provide the architectural setting of common worship. The term liturgical architecture indicates the chief function of the buildings we are to consider in the remaining chapters of this book.

II
Principles of Liturgical Architecture

We have spoken in some detail in the first chapter of the two concepts of worship dominant in American Protestantism today: worship approached primarily as a matter of feeling and worship conceived of as basically work performed in God's service. We can best apply these approaches to our consideration of architecture by analyzing those elements of a building calculated to affect the feelings, the emotive factors, and then discussing the parts of the building used in performing the work of worship, the liturgical factors.

The emotive factors are those which are primarily directed toward arousing and maintaining certain emotions. They seek to produce an effect on the worshiper in order that he might receive a certain experience from having worshiped. Frequently this is done by creating an atmosphere with the intention of inducing a mood in the mind of the worshiper.

On the other hand, the liturgical factors seek to provide tools and space for the performance of worship. The concern here is with work done rather than experiences felt. The liturgical factors involve action, and this is reflected in their use for doing the work of worship.

I

Though we rarely think about it, every building we encounter elicits from us some response, especially when we enter it. There is a feeling of quiet charm that we may experience upon entering a home, a sense of cleanliness and efficiency radiated by a dentist's office, and the attractive abundance of a supermarket. Most of these impressions are so familiar we hardly pause to remark about them. If we rarely visit large railway or airport terminals we may be struck by their vastness when we do. A similar experience awaits us in huge sports arenas and auditoriums. Consciously or unconsciously, the interiors make an impression upon us.

Rarely do we stop to examine the emotive factors to which we respond. In the case of vast arenas part of the basis for our reaction may be obvious. The magnitude of the space enclosed is overwhelming. But size is only one of the factors that elicits our response. We react to a building as a whole, not simply to individual aspects of it. Our response is to all that the senses detect —color, lighting, proportion, texture, and other factors—just as in eating cake we taste the blend of all the ingredients, not sugar or flour alone. It is important to remember that we encounter the emotive factors as a totality, not each one separately. It is only when we stop to analyze the emotive factors that we become aware of each of them as distinct from other items.

In many cases the responses which buildings draw from us are not accidental. A business firm is particularly concerned that its offices should produce an image of progressiveness and reliability. To achieve these impressions emotive factors have been carefully analyzed. Indeed, helping firms create a corporate image has become a highly specialized occupation.

Modern architecture has produced a fantastic variety of techniques for creating emotive factors. Lighting is one of the most important of these. Natural light can be admitted through wide expanses of glass, colored by glass, or bounced off certain surfaces. The possibilities of artificial lighting are even more varied. Some areas may be pinpointed, others flooded with light. Intensity can be changed with the turn of a knob.

The possibilities of the use of color are no less extensive. Color is one of the most important emotive factors available. No longer are churches limited to dark oak paneling. All the colors of the rainbow can be used to stimulate responses. An equally wide selection of textures is possible. Along with the traditional building materials—wood, brick, stone, and plaster—we now have in common use these materials in new forms plus synthetic materials.

Of even more direct emotive content is the matter of proportions. Gothic vaulting could not span an area wider than eighty feet without intervening supports. Today the dimensions of a church are more apt to be determined by the space needed than by structural limitations. Great height can be encompassed with the same ease as width and length. As emotive factors, proportions can be used in a variety of ways. Perhaps none of them are quite as forceful as excessive height.

All these emotive factors and many others are used by churches today in order to elicit desired responses. Building committees are inclined to spend a great deal of time in discussions of these factors. Essentially, the intention is described by the often-used phrase, "creating a worshipful atmosphere."

What is a "worshipful atmosphere"? The question is a difficult one to answer, particularly since the answers vary considerably from individual to individual. What one person calls a worshipful atmosphere is likely to strike another quite differently. It is obvious that a so-called worshipful atmosphere is largely a matter of personal opinion. For some the term suggests the "dim religious light" of Milton's cloister in *Il Penseroso*. They delight in the accumulated shadows of high roofs, windows that admit little or only colored light, and dark recesses. For others quite an opposite effect is demanded. They associate clear, well-defined space, brightly lighted, with worship. There are multitudes of irrational prejudices which also effect the desired response. People have been known to oppose the use of a certain color in a church because it was the favorite color of a mother-in-law.

This strongly suggests that association is a very powerful constituent of a worshipful atmosphere. People associate the feelings they have had at worship with the building where they had these experiences. When they move to another community they instinctively desire the same type of surroundings in order to produce the same feelings. Those who have been accustomed to a "dim religious light" equate it with a worshipful atmosphere. Those who have been used to a white Georgian interior associate worship with a well-lighted building.

As can be seen, this does not make it easy to secure a consensus of the necessary components for a worshipful atmosphere. Yet it does show the persistency of the demand for a church to *look* "like a church," that is, the church a person knows best. There seem to be but few constants in creating a worshipful atmosphere. Bright or dim light, soothing or brilliant colors, rough or fine textures, all these and many more find their proponents. Indeed, about the only real constant seems to be a demand for extra height. With remarkable unanimity people seem to associate an unusually high interior with worship and to reject low ceilings or roofs as not conducive to worship.

The emotive factors play a very important role in arousing the feelings often associated with personal devotions. It is for this reason that concern with regard to the emotive factors is justified. A sense of beauty, whether man-made or natural, can greatly contribute to personal devotions by stimulating the feelings. The reaction of the twelfth-century Abbot Suger to the great gothic church of St.-Denis and its ornaments is illustrative. "When—out of my delight in the beauty of the house of God . . . worthy meditation has induced me to reflect, transferring that which is material to that which is immaterial . . . it seems to me . . . that, by the grace of God, I can be transported from this inferior to that higher world in an anagogical manner." [1]

However important the emotive factors may be in church building, they do present some very real problems. As has been pointed out, responses to these factors vary so tremendously that it is difficult to erect a building which all worshipers will consider worshipful. There is also the danger of too much concern about how a building looks. It must be remembered that, in addition to its other attributes, a building is a functioning unit and like a machine must be judged by how efficient and economical it is to construct and operate. There is frequently a danger that building committees become so enamored with an elegant façade or interior elevation that they forget the technical demands on the buildings. Ventilation, acoustics, and maintenance problems may seem mundane, but they are important.

Even deeper than this difficulty lies the fact that too much concentration upon the emotive factors has frequently obscured similar concern with the liturgical factors in church building. It should be remembered that although Protestant churches are used at times for personal devotions, their primary function is for common worship. There are a few types of buildings erected chiefly for personal devotions, for example, hospital chapels, meditation rooms, memorial chapels, and private oratories. But these are erected for exceptional purposes, whereas the usual Protestant church building is intended first of all for common worship. Recently Protestants have encouraged the use of churches for personal devotions, but the response has been negligible.

It is strange then that so much attention in building projects is devoted to emotive factors and comparatively so little concern

[1] *Abbot Suger on the Abbey Church of St.-Denis and Its Art Treasures,* edited, translated, and annotated by Erwin Panofsky (Princeton: Princeton University Press, 1946), pp. 63-5.

shown about how the building functions in common worship. One hears and reads much more about how new churches look than about how they work. This is true of most of the literature now available on church building. The emotive factors are discussed at length but the liturgical factors are virtually ignored. Surely this is putting the cart before the horse if we remember the main purpose for which churches are built!

There is a further irony. Churches built with careful and deliberate consideration of the liturgical factors have often been highly successful with the emotive factors, though the latter received less attention.

II

The liturgical factors, then, deserve the most serious attention in church building programs, though all too often they fail to receive it. This in itself is a bit strange, for historically, Protestants have placed great emphasis on the actions of worship. The liturgical factors, of course, are directly concerned with the doing of the work of worship. Indeed, the traditional Protestant tendency has been to think of worship and its settings in dynamic terms of action rather than in terms of place or substance. The Westminster Directory (1644), the traditional standard for Presbyterian worship, stated that "no place is capable of any holiness." [2] To the Westminster divines it was unthinkable that holiness should be attributed to physical things in and of themselves. On the other hand, they were equally firm in their conviction that "preaching of the word" is "the power of God unto salvation, and one of the greatest and most excellent works belonging to the ministry of the Gospel." [3] The writers of the Scotch Confes-

[2] *Reliquiae Liturgicae: Documents Connected with the Liturgy of the Church of England,* edited by Peter Hall (Bath: Binns and Goodwin, 1847), III, 82.

[3] Ibid. III, 35.

sion of Faith (1560) utterly denied the suggestion that the sacraments were "nathing ellis bot naked and baire signes." [4] It was
only through the actions performed with them that physical objects became significant. Thus while reformer after reformer
could fulminate against the superstitious use made by Roman
Catholics of objects and places (holy places, holy wells, consecrated ground, and the reserved sacrament), the Protestant never
doubted that the acts which were performed in his own worship,
using physical objects all the while, were anything less than
sacred. The function of things may be sacred even though they
possess no sanctity of themselves. There is nothing sacred about
a pulpit or font to a Protestant, but there is definitely something
sacred in preaching or baptism, the acts for which these objects
are employed. In this sense function is a very important consideration with respect to every bit of furnishing or space in a
church.

As mentioned before, the nature of common worship is that of
work done together as a congregation. The liturgical factors of a
building are simply the provisions which are made for this work.
In simplest terms they are concerned with the tools provided and
the space allotted for this work. It is useful, though not necessary,
to have these tools and space provided, for obviously common
worship can be conducted without a building. Preaching can
occur anywhere and baptism can be performed in any stream.
Yet certain furnishings and uses of space give greater convenience in the performance of common worship.

As with any tools or space utilized, it is crucial to know what
purpose they serve in order to design them correctly. Before a
church can be designed fundamental questions must be raised
about the purpose of the church building and all its contents. It is
not enough to say it is built for common worship. A congrega-

[4] *Creeds of Christendom with a History and Critical Notes,* edited by Philip
Schaff (New York: Harper and Brothers, 1919), III, 468.

tion or its building committee must ask questions about the purpose of every act performed in its worship before it can give sufficient instruction to the architect and designers. This means that first and last the problems of church architecture are theological ones. The responsibility for raising these questions and for providing at least tentative answers rests upon the congregation, not upon the architect. Indeed a congregation is in no position to engage an architect until it has discussed the theological questions of what the Church is and what it does when it gathers for common worship. These are not easy questions. Indeed, they are among the most basic problems of theology. But unless a congregation is willing to weigh these questions (which it ought to be asking itself constantly whether it be planning to build or not) it can hardly expect an adequate building, no matter how competent the architect may be.

Basically, the questions that must be raised deal with the being and purpose of the Church. These questions will not be settled in a few meetings. Theologians have not come to a consensus on them in almost two thousand years. But the very act of posing these questions promises the possibility of renewal in the life of the congregation. Many congregations that have made the effort to answer these theological questions in preparation for building have found the occasion a great opportunity for the renewal of their life as a community of faith. Without such an effort, adequate church building is an impossibility. The architect can only copy the mistakes of others unless the congregation can present him with a well-thought-out statement on the nature of the Church and a detailed explanation of the meaning of every act performed in its common worship. Obviously such statements will differ from congregation to congregation, inasmuch as there are no two congregations whose worship is identical, even within the same denomination. In the long run the act of preparing such statements may be more significant in the life of the congregation than the building itself. Indeed, it is conceivable that such discussions may lead to the conclusion that a building is not necessary.

It is our purpose here to show some of the central concerns which will arise when this type of questioning has occurred and is directed particularly to the liturgical factors. In concrete terms these concerns are directed to questions about the liturgical centers and liturgical spaces. The liturgical centers are those furnishings which provide a focus for the various acts of work performed in common worship. They are important because they are where something is *done*. Usually they include the pulpit, possibly a lectern or various forms of reading desks, prayer desks or litany desks, the baptismal font or baptistery (baptismal tank), and the altar-table with its rails and credence table. The liturgical spaces, on the other hand, are areas of the building set aside for the performance of particular acts of worship which may or may not demand the use of liturgical centers. The liturgical spaces include the location of the congregation, the location of the choir, aisles and passages for processions, baptismal space, and altar-table space.

As can readily be seen, these centers and spaces do little to create a mood or atmosphere. Processional space, for example, may simply be empty space; the altar-table may simply be a slab of wood on which things are placed. But they do have a great importance because of their function. Each has definite uses in common worship, yet if all were omitted a building's worshipful atmosphere might remain unchanged. Without them a church could still be used for personal devotions, but it would be found most inconvenient for common worship. Liturgical centers and liturgical spaces are provided for the performance of specific acts, the acts of common worship.

It is not without reason that the pulpit has been the chief liturgical center in most Protestant churches. Its prime function, of course, has been to provide the necessities for preaching: a platform to elevate the preacher so that he can be seen and heard, a ledge to hold his Bible and manuscript, and perhaps a sounding board or microphone to increase his audibility. During days of persecution a portable pulpit provided the only church facility available for French Protestants. The pulpit was carried about from one hiding place to another and the worshipers gathered about it to hear God's Word. In a sense this is characteristic of Protestantism, for most of the major denominations have always had a very exalted view of preaching.[5]

In the early days of the Reformation, Luther stressed the importance of preaching, insisting, "The Christian congregation never should assemble unless God's Word is preached and prayer is made, no matter for how brief a time this may be." [6] Calvin was no less insistent, maintaining that even holy communion needs preaching, "For whatever benefit may come to us from the Supper requires the Word: whether we are to be confirmed in faith, or exercised in confession, or aroused to duty, there is need of preaching." [7] Preaching was to accompany each service of common worship. Preaching is prescribed at holy communion in the *Book of Common Prayer* and is central in the worship of Baptists, Congregationalists, and Presbyterians. Methodism began as a preaching movement.

Why has preaching been so important in Protestantism? Primarily because most Protestants see preaching as dependent upon the power of God. It is not intended to be an inspiring talk or even an exciting challenge to action presented by the minister on

[5] Cf. James A. Whyte, "A Place for the Preaching of the Word," *Church-building*, #9 (1963), 5–11.

[6] "Concerning the Ordering of Divine Worship in the Congregation," *Works of Martin Luther* (Philadelphia edition; Philadelphia: Muhlenberg Press, 1932), VI, 60.

[7] *Calvin: Institutes of the Christian Religion*, IV, xvii, 39, translated by Ford L. Battles and edited by John T. McNeill (Philadelphia: Westminster, 1960), II, 1416.

his own authority. Preaching in Protestantism has been seen as a means by which the power of God is made present in the midst of His people. God's acts on the behalf of His people are recalled and again made present by their saving power. Thus, though preaching deals with events past, it is never remote in time for the power of God is present in the recital of these events. In the recital of these actions God is acting in our midst, the preacher being his agent.

When Paul says that "we preach Christ crucified" he might add that Christ is not only the subject of the sermon but the power which makes it possible. Preaching does not come about through the minister's personality and scholarship, though God uses these talents, but through God addressing His people in, with, and under the words of the preacher. There is a real paradox here, for it seems strange that Almighty God should entrust His Word to sinful men, to "earthen vessels." Yet the whole story of the incarnation is that of God entering history in the person of a man. And that incarnation continues every time the preacher goes into the pulpit and his words become the vehicle of God's Eternal Word. The sermon becomes a means by which God's saving power is made contemporary to every hearer.

In this sense the pulpit has a very sacred function. It is not a stand provided for a bit of oratory but veritably the throne of the Word of God. In the early Church the sermon was often preached by the bishop sitting upon his throne. The pulpit in most Protestant churches is a significant liturgical center. There is every reason to make it prominent rather than inconspicuous. Some pulpits are more successful than others in echoing the note of authority found in preaching, authority which is of God, not of man.

In many churches the pulpit has uses other than preaching. Sometimes the entire service is conducted from the pulpit. This has the advantage of simplicity but, since it indicates that every part of the service from announcements to benediction is the same act, it does lead to confusion. There is much to be said for movements in which the minister (and other worshipers) go from one liturgical center or space to another as the acts of worship progress. Ideally the pulpit is the liturgical center from which the Bible lessons are read, the minister leads the congregation in the Creed, and the Word is preached. These are the acts that center in the proclamation of the Word. Acts of praise and sacrifice might better take place elsewhere, and the movement of the preacher to the pulpit is in itself a statement of the change in the nature of the acts performed.

Closely related to the pulpit are a variety of other liturgical centers which may or may not appear in churches. These are the lectern, reading desk, and various types of prayer desks and litany desks. Their function is to hold the Bible or service books while being read in the service. Frequently an entire service of worship (when the sacraments are not celebrated) may be read from a lectern except for the sermon. The prayer desks and litany desks, as their names indicate, are used for prayers and litanies, the minister kneeling at these liturgical centers.

Some serious questions ought to be raised about each liturgical center. The lectern, now so common in many Protestant churches, was introduced in the nineteenth century, which copied it from the Middle Ages. Often it is used to balance a pulpit at the other side of the chancel. But why should the reading of the lessons be separated from the preaching of the Word? Indeed, placing the Bible on a lectern apart from the pulpit suggests that the sources and authority of printed Word and preached Word are different. Would it not be better to have the Word read from the same spot where it is expounded? It would be wise, when possible, to have the Bible visible on the pulpit when in use. This may be done with a two-sided stand with the Old Testament on one side and the New Testament on the other. Thus whichever Testament is being read, the other faces the congregation. In the Church of Scotland a ceremony of bringing the

Bible to the pulpit precedes the reading and preaching of the Word. The lectern is not an essential liturgical center and could be dispensed with in many cases.

The need for prayer desks and litany desks is also open to question. In form they are often similar to the *prie-dieu*, the kneeler and book rest used for personal devotions. They tend to suggest that the minister is offering his devotions to which the congregation is an audience. Would it not be better for the minister to stand behind the altar-table, facing the people, to join in offering their sacrifice of praise and thanksgiving? The standing position, of course, was the position for public prayer in the early Church. The altar-table has always been the liturgical center at which offerings have been made. Calvin evidently preferred to perform the entire service except for the sermon from behind the altar-table. There is much to be said for this position. It indicates that minister and people are one in the prayers offered to God. It also undercuts the unfortunate tendency to make of pastoral prayers sermonettes addressed to the congregation rather than to God.

Reading desks have often combined the functions of lecterns and prayer desks, plus such an obsolete practice as a clerk's reading out the lines of psalms and hymns when the people did not have hymnbooks. The same criticisms apply to reading desks. Their functions could be better performed at other more important liturgical centers.

It is important today to stress the essentials in worship rather than the nonessentials. This is a time for purification—not elaboration—in worship. This is also true of the liturgical centers. Those that are not vital should be removed. They often add needless complication to the acts performed in worship by necessitating movements that are not significant and concealing those that are. It would be better to concentrate on the essential liturgical centers.

The baptismal font or baptistery is certainly one of the essentials. Its function is clear-cut. It serves as the container for the water of baptism. Other than that it has no function. The forms differ depending upon the mode of baptisms—pouring, sprinkling, or immersion. If only infants are to be immersed the size will vary tremendously from that necessary for adult immersion. But the purpose remains the same: font and baptistery are essentially containers for the water used in baptism.

The questions we raise about this liturgical center depend basically upon our theology of baptism. Here there is variety within Christendom. In general it can be said that baptism is seen as involving a new relationship between the baptized person and Christ, and those in Christ's Church. The chief division lies between those who see baptism as a sign of this relationship, making it apparent, and those who see baptism as in some manner initiating the new relationship. Even within the same denomination one can find theologians disagreeing on the meaning of baptism. Karl Barth argues that baptism is a making known of a salvation already experienced, a *"cognitio salutis,"* which does not add anything to that which the believer has, but makes it public.[8] Hence, Barth maintains only adults should be baptized. On the other hand, Oscar Cullmann maintains that in baptism an infant is placed within the Church which is the realm of salvation. Thus he is placed within a new relationship to Christ and fellow Christians by being united to the body of Christ.[9] For Cullmann, baptism anticipates faith, which is given by the Holy Spirit within the Church.

Other aspects of baptism are present too. For some it is seen as accompanying the forgiveness of sins, "sins original or added" being erased in baptism, according to Augustine. Others see in it an act of dedication by which the parents promise to rear the child in the Christian faith. Most Christians agree that baptism

[8] *The Teaching of the Church Regarding Baptism,* translated by Ernest A. Payne (London: S.C.M., 1948), p. 27.

[9] *Baptism in the New Testament,* translated by J. K. S. Reid (London: S.C.M., 1950), p. 54.

makes one a member of the Church though some have other services which confirm this at an age of maturity. Some press the
idea of baptism as a new birth in which the child, having been
born physically of his mother, is now born spiritually into a new
body, the body of Christ. Roman Catholics even speak of the
font as a womb. Paul saw baptism as a participation in the death
and resurrection of Christ, acts repeated in the descent into the
water and in being raised afterward. By no means do these exhaust the interpretations of baptism nor are these doctrines mu-
tually exclusive. It is vital though that a congregation come to a
deep understanding of this sacrament in order to understand the
function of a font or baptistery.

In some churches the most prominent liturgical center is the
altar-table. Not only does it function as the center of the holy
communion but also as an important part of the setting for all
worship. The altar-table signifies what is offered to God (altar)
as well as what is given to man (table). Neither term alone indicates the purpose of this liturgical center. The altar-table can be
used as the place at which prayer and acts of praise are offered
to God in any service of worship. It also functions as the center
from which an offering can be made of our weekday work in the
form of money. Long before Christian times altars were used to
receive the gifts of man's work in which worshipers offered
themselves to God through these tokens. A table recalls God's
supreme giving of Himself to man in the Christ, and the fellowship thereby inaugurated. The recalling of these events is the
very center of the Christian life of worship. The Lord's supper,
holy communion, eucharist, mass, call it what we will, here is the
very heart of Christian worship. In no other service is there so
dramatic an expression of the work of worship done in common
by all those worshiping.

The Protestant reformers desired, for the most part, that the
holy communion be celebrated frequently. Calvin desired a
weekly celebration, and Cranmer showed some preference for a

daily one, but only when the priest had "some that will communicate with hym." Early Methodism placed a great emphasis on frequent communion, which Wesley called a duty. This emphasis on frequent communion decreased in most Protestant denominations but it is gradually reappearing in our own time. Many congregations have moved from a quarterly celebration to a monthly one. Others have changed to even more frequent celebrations. There is every indication that this tendency will continue. The altar-table which was once used only three or four times a year for holy communion now becomes a more important item than in the recent past.

The concepts held regarding the holy communion dictate to a great extent any discussion of the function of this particular liturgical center. As with baptism, it is impossible to exhaust the meaning of the sacrament of holy communion. Many concepts are held concerning the Lord's supper and have often provoked bitter theological controversy within Christendom. Surprisingly, many of these concepts are not opposed to each other and probably the best approach is a comprehensive one which realizes that various interpretations belong together. The outline here follows the discussion by Yngve Brilioth, a Swedish Lutheran theologian, in his book *Eucharistic Faith and Practice*.[10]

Brilioth analyzes the most significant interpretations of the holy communion under five headings. First of all, he points out that one of the traditional names, the eucharist, implies that the service is fundamentally an act of thanksgiving. Strong overtones of thanksgiving appear in all liturgies from earliest times to the present. A strong theme in the Lord's supper has been the fellowship of those sharing in the meal. This communion fellowship finds its supreme expression in the acts which are performed together in the sacrament. It is also a service with a historical aspect, which commemorates not only the events of the last supper but

[10] Translated by A. G. Hebert (London: S.P.C.K., 1930).

the whole history of salvation. As in preaching, the events of salvation history with their saving power are again made contemporary. According to Dom Odo Casel, the Christian mystery concerns the reality of these events made again present through being re-enacted.[11] There is also a strong note of sacrifice in the holy communion. The one sacrifice of Christ on the cross is recalled and the Church is united to Christ in His eternal offering of Himself. Protestants are gradually becoming more aware of the importance of the concept of sacrifice without its medieval accretions. Finally there is a strong sense in which the Lord's supper mediates the presence of the Lord Himself. Though theological battles have been fought over the manner in which Christ is present, few have cared to deny that He is somehow present through the sacrament. This list does not exhaust the aspects of the sacrament but suggests interpretations that must be considered by those providing an architectural setting for it.

Frequently the altar-table is accompanied by other furnishings, especially altar rails and a credence table. The rails date from a rather late time, the sixteenth century, and seem to have been introduced largely to define a liturgical space. They also served to protect the altar-table from profanation. Whether this protection is now necessary is questionable. Certainly it is possible to kneel without the support of the rails, and the custom in some churches of placing communion glasses on the back of the rails could be avoided by collecting them or by using a common cup. The credence table is used to hold the communion elements until needed in the service. It is quite possible, however, that it need not be in the immediate vicinity of the altar-table and might be better located somewhere in the midst of or behind the congregation so that these gifts might dramatically be brought forward to the altar-table as an offering during the service itself.

[11] *The Mystery of Christian Worship and Other Writings,* edited by Burkhard Neunheuser (Westminster, Md.: Newman, 1962), pp. 50–62.

The liturgical centers revolve around three essentials: pulpit, font, and altar-table. Although these may be accompanied by liturgical centers of secondary importance, they have only minor functions in themselves and may detract from the primary centers.

It is difficult to be as explicit about liturgical space as liturgical centers since space is not always so clearly defined by function in a church. The items defining space are apt to be a bit nebulous at times. It may be a rise in the floor level, the presence or absence of pews or chairs, enclosure by rails or screens, or the use of galleries. Lighting can be used effectively today to define space by changing the intensity of light or shadow. Even light fixtures can be used to mark off space. Thus churches are organized into liturgical spaces, though they may not be so obvious as the liturgical centers.

Most important of these is the place where the congregation sits, stands, or kneels. In most churches this space is defined by the presence of pews or chairs. Indeed this is the most important liturgical space, for much of the action of common worship is performed by the congregation (hymns, prayers) though many church buildings ignore this fact. Among Quakers, congregational space is the only liturgical space in the building. In most churches the acts of the congregation vary according to the type of service. This makes it preferable to have some flexibility in the liturgical space occupied by the congregation which is not always possible with fixed pews. Movable chairs may give this flexibility and (if well chosen) still have the beauty associated with pews. Seating must also be provided for the clergy. In some cases this may be a part of the congregational space.

The choir occupies a liturgical space which may or may not be separate from that occupied by the congregation. This space is usually filled with seating plus accommodation for an organ console. At present there is considerable uncertainty about the functions of the choir in Protestant worship. As a result of this uncertainty the purposes served by this liturgical space are not always easy to define. (Some of these problems will be discussed in Chapter VII.)

Processional space also serves a liturgical function. Most Protestants are inclined to think of processions as something exclusively Roman Catholic, yet many Protestant services have a choir procession and almost all have an offertory procession. Nevertheless, those taking part in the procession are not usually the congregation. There are a few congregations where the entire congregation goes to the altar-table to offer their gifts. In many denominations the people go to the altar rails to receive communion or to kneel for prayer. In weddings and funerals processional space is particularly important.

Processional space, then, provides for movement from one liturgical space to another, such as from a pew to the space about the altar-table. Though this space is not always used during the service by all members of the congregation, it is used by their representatives. Thus it is important that processional space maintain a representative character, since the movement along the aisles and passages is representative of those occupying the pews. Each portion of the congregation should have immediate access to the chief liturgical centers. This does not mean a central aisle is the only answer, though frequently it is the most obvious one.

In some denominations, occasional processions may involve the movement of the entire congregation around the building. On these occasions the perimeter of the building is encompassed usually and the liturgical centers of the chapels and the main church visited.

Special liturgical space is often provided for the font or baptistery. Professor J. G. Davies argues most persuasively for such space in *The Architectural Setting of Baptism.*[12] Not only is

---

[12] (London: Barrie and Rockliff, 1962), p. 166.

space necessary for the font itself, but in many cases space must be provided for parents, candidates, sponsors, and clergy. In cases in which the baptistery is a tank considerable space will be needed, since provision must be made for the tank, steps, and access to private rooms where the candidates may change their clothes. Even where a font is used, adequate space is necessary.

We are more accustomed to having the space about the altar-table well defined. This space is often referred to as the sanctuary. In many churches, altar rails and changes in floor level make the boundaries of the sanctuary very definite. In some churches this is the most conspicuous space in the building. Here may be performed many of the acts of every service of worship, particularly those centering in prayer, praise, and offering. Since such a variety of functions must be performed, considerable space is necessary, especially when there is more than one minister. This space is the center of the acts of the Lord's supper, the taking of bread and wine, blessing them, breaking the bread, and giving them to the people. Frequently today sanctuaries are designed so that a larger number of people can receive communion at the same time. In some denominations, to be sure, this takes place in the pews. Many denominations, however, prefer to maintain the action of going to the altar-table space, an act which in itself expresses both offering and receiving. In order to avoid excessive waits it has been found better to make this space accessible from more than one side.

Liturgical spaces include the place where the congregation does its work, the place for the choir's work, processional space, space about the font or baptistery, and that about the altar-table. Awareness of the functions of the liturgical spaces and the liturgical centers is absolutely essential in planning an adequate building for common worship.

III

Two matters are of particular importance in discussing the liturgical factors: the design of the liturgical centers, and the arrangement of the liturgical centers and liturgical spaces.

The design of the liturgical centers is important because it can express the concepts of worship held by the congregation. Few groups would knowingly build a church which flouted their beliefs, yet many, through ignorance, have done this. Obviously many have been speaking in an unfamiliar tongue here, and unblushingly and unknowingly have erred in their grammar.

The design of the pulpit can give a sense of the divine-human encounter possible in preaching. This is especially true when the pulpit is solid and substantial enough to suggest authority far higher than the preacher's personality.

The font or baptistery by its design reflects a concept of Christian initiation. For the immersion of adults a baptistery that can be filled with water is necessary. A font suffices for sprinkling or pouring or for immersing a baby. Often the size of the font is a good indication of how important this sacrament is in the life of the congregation. When nothing is provided but a small brass or glass basin one cannot help wondering whether the sacrament is really accorded the respect it deserves. If the method of pouring is used (often with a baptismal shell) it will be necessary to have the font large enough to catch the drippings. Indeed this "laver of regeneration" is much more dramatic when the water can be seen and heard.

The chief liturgical center for the holy communion and other acts of worship, the altar-table, has been the subject of enduring controversy both as to materials (stone vs. wood) or form (altar vs. table). Actually this liturgical center serves as both an altar of sacrifice and a table of fellowship.

From these few examples it can be seen that the design of the liturgical centers can be an important means of making manifest our beliefs about worship. This is not merely a matter of taste but a means of showing forth definite theological concepts.

The arrangement of the liturgical centers and liturgical spaces in relation to each other is equally important. Usually the best way to analyze the function of a building is by looking at its floor plan. This will reveal much that cannot be learned from simply looking at the façade. Too often, congregations decide on the merits of a building project by looking at a rendering of the façade or an interior elevation rather than at the floor plan. Just as a floor plan tells us more about how livable a house is than a photograph of the exterior does, so a floor plan helps us to determine the merits of a scheme for a church. Floor plans can be easily sketched with the location of liturgical centers and spaces marked by letters. Then one is in a position to judge the project and how it is intended to function. Without a floor plan this is very difficult.

In analyzing the relative positions of the liturgical centers and spaces we soon realize that they have definite meanings. Far too often mistakes made here have unexpectedly warped a congregation's concepts of worship or eliminated the possibility of their full participation in it. Instead of their beliefs about worship determining their building, the edifice has, for better or worse, determined their concepts of worship. This silent influence is often difficult or impossible to refute, especially after living with it for a long time.

In many churches built in the last forty years the liturgical space allotted to the congregation is arranged to suggest that the congregation is an audience which watches the clergy and choir perform the acts of worship. Yet the opposite should be the case, for the congregation are actors in common worship. A way must be found to gather the congregation about the liturgical centers and spaces so that they realize they are the performers with their own work to do, not passive spectators.

Where to locate the choir is often puzzling, owing to the uncertainty about its function in Protestant common worship. Recent experiments reflect a trend to rethinking the question of the choir's basic purpose.

As already indicated, processional space is liturgical space, for some of the significant movements in worship occur in this area. It is thus appropriate that processional space should connect the various liturgical centers and spaces while expressing a representative character for the congregation. Consideration should also be given to the fact that it is through this space that the congregation disperses to perform its work in the world.

The position of the pulpit creates special problems. Not only must the preacher be heard by all his congregation but he should be seen by them as well. This means that by turning his head but slightly the preacher should be able to look every member of the congregation in the eye. The eye is a means of communication as well as the voice, a fact known to any new parent. Once a baby loses sight of a person, he is lost completely. Pulpits placed at the center of round churches make preaching exceedingly difficult.

The arrangement of baptismal space is largely determined by the concept of this sacrament. If baptism is interpreted as a public profession of faith, it certainly must be performed in a conspicuous position before the congregation. If, however, baptism is regarded as a family act of dedication, the baptismal space may be somewhat secluded for a private ceremony. This practice seems to be decreasing. In some denominations the font appears near the entrance to the church and suggests that baptism is the means of entering the Christian Church. There are signs that this position is now less frequent, partly because most churches today have several entrances (due to fire laws, if nothing else), but more significantly because baptism is an act of worship in which the entire congregation joins. Frequently today fonts are set up before the congregation, sometimes at the entrance to the sanctuary.

The arrangement of the altar-table space has been subject to much dispute. The tendency now is to place the sanctuary near the laity. Sometimes the congregational space completely surrounds the altar-table. Though the clergy have special functions to perform at the altar-table, the whole congregation assembles as the family of God about the Lord's table. The altar-table space is used by the clergy to minister to the congregation, and barriers of steps, screens, and rails between congregational space and sanctuary are disappearing.

It should be stressed that the relative positions of the liturgical centers and spaces are very important. Too often there has been a tendency to give an either/or effect between pulpit and altar-table. There is an underlying unity between the Word made present in preaching and the Word visible in the sacrament. The problem is to find a visual relationship which stresses this underlying unity.

The problems of the design of liturgical centers and the arrangement of centers and spaces have not been exhausted in this survey. However, some of the basic liturgical factors have been underlined. It is hoped that this will show the great need for careful analysis of these factors, far more important in common worship than the emotive factors. Unfortunately, this type of analysis has hitherto been the exception rather than the rule. As a result, the majority of churches built in the last few years in America are monuments of confusion in their function in common worship.

The next four chapters show the varieties of buildings that have been used by Christians since churches were first built. Many congregations hesitate to embark upon experiments, not realizing how frequent experimentation has been in the past. None of the examples cited are meant for slavish imitation. But they demonstrate both some of the possibilities and some of the blind alleys which are present to church builders today. No perfect church has ever been built; even if it were to be built, modifications in concepts of worship would in time make it less than ideal.

The most important consideration is first to ask the right theological questions and then to have the courage to follow the implications with both consistency and common sense. The following chapters show that others have done this in many widely differing historical contexts.

III
Early and Medieval Patterns

In this and the following three chapters we shall examine some of the experiments in liturgical architecture which have taken place through the centuries. Our primary concern will be with the liturgical factors that have affected the design of churches. Most of our attention will be devoted to the design and location of the liturgical centers and their relationship to the various liturgical spaces of the buildings involved. By no means is this intended to be an exhaustive study, but it should be an indication of the constancy of experimentation, and suggest some of the possibilities open to church builders today.

The history of liturgical architecture is one of slow but constant change, reflecting developments in worship itself. Thus we can trace changing patterns in worship in new forms of church buildings. Our purpose is to consider how these changes in worship have found expression in architecture throughout the history of the Church. This information can help us design churches for contemporary worship, profiting from the advances of other ages while remaining aware of the inadequacies for our time of their solutions. Changes in church architecture are the result of mutation rather than a steady line of evolution.

It should be made clear that our purpose in this and the next three chapters is not to give a history of Christian church architecture. Such material can be found in the books listed in the bibliography. Rather our concern is to select liturgical arrangements of particular interest. Some of these were widely adopted; others were only isolated experiments. Our purpose is to discuss a selected number of the most interesting examples, not to give a comprehensive or representative survey.

The floor plans which accompany the text are simply diagrams used to illustrate various liturgical arrangements. They are not necessarily drawn to scale and are only meant to show relationships. The symbols used include: A, altar-table; P, pulpit; L, lectern, or D, reading desk; F, font; and C, choir. Galleries are indicated by dotted lines. In many cases only the main space of the building is depicted.

I

Our information about the church buildings of the first three centuries of the Christian era is indeed scanty. It must be remembered that during this period the Church was subject to frequent persecution and for much of the time Christian worship had to be conducted in secret. However, within the Roman Empire there were periods during which it was possible to construct churches even before the persecution ceased in A.D. 313. Many of these were destroyed in subsequent persecutions.

In this early period our attention is directed instead to the Church which met in the homes of various Christians. Frequently this meant meeting for worship in secrecy, the worshipers coming together despite the threat of death from the state and the ever-present danger that mobs, associating Christian worship with all manner of crimes, would attack the worshipers. To assemble for Christian worship might literally involve the sacrifice of one's life. It is not surprising that the worship of the early Christians reflects a strong sense of personal involvement reflected by participation in the actions of the liturgy in a most direct fashion.[1] It was inevitable that such groups were characterized by a strong corporate sense, and the small number present made worship intimate.

The architectural evidence of how homes were used for Christian worship is slight. Since many of the homes were lived in, the arrangements for worship would necessarily have to be easily concealed, particularly at times when even the possession of the Scriptures could be used as evidence against a person. Thus the ordinary furnishings of the home—a table, a chair—might be used for Christian worship. We have seen the same thing in our own time in lands where Christians are persecuted. Perhaps of even greater interest is the present-day use of the house-church in lands where Christianity is freely exercised but the need is felt for relating the life of the parish church more directly to the daily life of the families of the parish.[2]

There are several theories about the most common ways of using the homes of private citizens for worship during the days of persecution. Gregory Dix is of the opinion that the private home of a wealthy family of the second and third centuries was readily adapted for Christian worship.[3] In most cases these buildings surrounded a courtyard, the *atrium*, open at the top with a pool beneath to catch the rain. Beyond the courtyard was the *tablinum*, a reception room and shrine used in ceremonial func-

[1] For a dramatic reconstruction of worship as Christians in the second or third centuries conducted it, see Gregory Dix, *The Shape of the Liturgy* (Westminster: Dacre, 1945), Ch. VI. Dix's book is one of the most important of recent liturgical studies. See also six accounts of holy communion as it was conducted at different epochs in the history of the Church in Massey H. Shepherd's *"At All Times and in All Places"* (Greenwich: Seabury, 1953), of which Chapter I deals with the period of persecution.

[2] Cf. E. W. Southcott, *The Parish Comes Alive* (London: A. R. Mowbray, 1956), Ch. VI.

[3] *The Shape of the Liturgy*, pp. 22–3.

tions of the family. Before the *tablinum* was a table, and often a chair, used by the head of the family on ceremonial occasions, stood behind the table. Dix argued that this provided a ready-made setting for the Christian eucharist, the bishop sitting upon the chair surrounded by other ministers (the presbyters). According to Dix the table became the Christian altar-table and the pool in the *atrium* became the place of baptism in the midst of the congregation who gathered there. The vessels used could occasionally be of considerable magnificence as attested by the records still extant of a raid Roman officials made on a house-church in Cirta, North Africa, in A.D. 303.

This theory is open to serious question because of the lack of any archaeological evidence in its favor. It now seems more likely that special rooms were provided for the different acts of Christian worship, and that the *atrium* was not used at all for this purpose. The *atrium* would be rather conspicuous in times of persecution and not particularly comfortable in inclement weather. It seems more probable that the larger rooms of the house, especially the formal dining room, or space provided by knocking out the wall between two smaller rooms, became the scene of the eucharist. Other rooms might be adapted for the baptistery, for the church supper (the agape), as classrooms for those who were learning the faith, and for accommodations for the clergy.[4]

The best preserved example of a house-church seems to substantiate this theory. In Dura-Europos, a Roman garrison town on the Euphrates River, a home (Figure 1) was adapted for a church in the early third century and destroyed about A.D. 256. The ruins indicate that a wall had been removed (broken line) and two rooms joined to provide space for the eucharistic as-

[4] For floor plans and drawings see J. G. Davies, *The Origin and Development of Early Christian Church Architecture* (New York: Philosophical Library, 1953), and Basil Minchin, *Outward and Visible* (London: Darton, Longman & Todd, 1961).

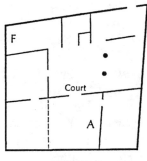

FIGURE 1

sembly. At one end appears a small platform, possibly for the altar-table or bishop's throne. A room at the opposite side of the house, likewise opening off the *atrium*, was probably used as a baptistery with a font covered by a canopy and the walls ornamented with frescoes.[5] Thus early there is a most explicit allocation of space for different liturgical functions, a pattern continued in church building up to the present.

II

The fourth century marks the most significant change of status in the history of the Church. From a religion not authorized by the state and often persecuted by it, Christianity became a religion tolerated throughout the Empire, espoused by the Emperor Constantine himself, and established by subsequent emperors as the only legal religion. The consequences of the Church's having become respectable and legal were tremendous as far as worship was concerned. Now that the Church could conduct its services

[5] For illustrations of the baptistery, see F. Van der Meer and Christine Mohrmann, *Atlas of the Early Christian World* (London: Nelson, 1958), plates 72 and 403. This book contains a magnificent collection of illustrations of churches and their contents of the first six centuries of the Christian era.

openly, Christian worship became an activity of the general populace rather than that of a harassed group meeting in private.

At the same time the Church was suddenly endowed with sumptuous buildings, Constantine himself building nine churches in Rome and many others in Jerusalem, Bethlehem, and Constantinople. The worship offered in these magnificent buildings reflected the splendor and dignity which the ancient world expected of public occasions. It is not strange that the etiquette of the imperial court with all its Oriental magnificence should be reflected in the worship of the Church, especially when the worship of the Christian God superseded the cult of the emperor for many people.

An almost inevitable consequence was the loss of intimacy of the small Christian group. Increasingly the clergy performed the acts of worship, with the laity becoming more and more passive. According to Dix, "The corporate action of the Church disappeared, and what was left was a rite conducted chiefly by the prayers of the clergy, in which the people still made responses but had otherwise little part." [6]

The most characteristic type of church of this period is the basilica. The basilican arrangement, which has been preserved in a number of ancient churches, has become of interest to church builders in our own time. Scholars are not of one mind about the ultimate origins of the basilica, but evidently it came into prominence as the usual form for the Roman law courts. The design was derived from the Greek temple, which in turn was derived from the private houses of the Greeks.[7]

The civil basilica in the Roman Empire served much the same function as the county courthouse and the high school auditorium do in American towns. Basically it was a long hall with

[6] *The Shape of the Liturgy,* p. 319.

[7] Cf. J. G. Davies, *Origin and Development of Early Christian Church Architecture,* Ch. II.

outer aisles divided from the main space by parallel colonnades. Frequently at one end was a semicircular apse (extension) in which there was a platform with a throne for the benefit of the judge, who might be flanked by scribes. The main entrances were at the opposite end of the structure or at the side. This building type the Church made her own in the fourth century. Perhaps its dominant characteristic is that it was a long building, with a long central axis, and basically rectangular in shape. Hence it is often referred to as a longitudinal building, a description it shares with most churches in the West.

The Church made some changes, of course, in the furnishings but the building kept its dominant architectural characteristics for centuries (Figure 2). The bishop's throne replaced that of the

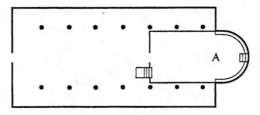

FIGURE 2

judge but retained the same central spot against the wall of the apse. It might be elevated at the head of several steps. The curve of the apse on either side of the bishop's throne contained a row of seats for the presbyters (ministers). The platform of the apse might extend out into the nave (the main hall of the church). Usually it was set off by a low screen (*cancellus*), thus defining and separating the liturgical space of the clergy from that of the laity. The altar-table appeared at the junction of the apse and nave though at times it stood even further out in the midst of the congregation.[8] At one side of the screen, projecting into the nave,

[8] Ibid. pp. 83–4, and Minchin, *Outward and Visible*, pp. 56–8.

was usually an ambo or lectern. The church sometimes included a narthex or porch at the entrance occupied by catechumens (those learning the faith) and penitents (those undergoing ecclesiastical discipline). Beyond this might appear an open court (*atrium*) with a fountain for symbolic cleansing of the hands and mouths of those entering the church to worship.

Basically each church had but few liturgical centers, and their functions were rather different from what we might expect. In the earliest period the altar-table was usually a table, resting upon one, three, four, or five legs, and quite distinct from the solid cube of the pagan altar. Usually the Christian altar-table was rather small, often almost square in shape, though some were possibly shaped like the letter "D," reflecting the banqueting table of the Romans. Beneath it might be a *confessio*, a repository for relics of martyrs and holy persons, and the whole might be given grandeur by a stone canopy (baldachino) above. In the first centuries the altar-table was always free-standing. The major clergy stood behind it, and the lesser clergy, singers, and congregation would stand in front and on either side of it. The bishop and presbyters celebrated the eucharist from behind the altar-table, facing the people (the so-called basilican position now being revived). It thus permitted a considerable intimacy and visibility. The communicants could easily stand about the altar-table to receive the elements. Most likely there was also a table or tables (the table of prothesis) at the eastern end of an aisle where the people placed their gifts of bread and wine at the offertory. Thus in a most dramatic fashion they made an offering of the fruits of their daily work.

Perhaps the next most important liturgical center was the bishop's throne or *cathedra*.[9] This was the place from which the

---

[9] Altar-tables, bishops' thrones, and ambos are illustrated in Van der Meer and Mohrmann, *Atlas of the Early Christian World*, plates 430–50. Cf. especially the illustration of Augustine's cathedral at Hippo (436) and the Church of St. Clement in Rome (430).

sermon was preached, the bishop seated according to the Jewish custom (Luke 4:20). The seated position signified teaching authority, and it was insisted that preaching was part of the bishop's liturgy, as he was representative of the tradition of the Church. Usually it was necessary for the throne to be raised by several steps or even a dozen (as at Torcello) so that the bishop might be visible to all as he preached. The presbyters were ranged on both sides of the bishop's throne. There may be a conscious repetition of this position of the clergy in the portrayal of God enthroned in heaven surrounded by a circle of seated elders in Revelation 4:2–4.

The ambo was an extension of the chancel platform. It was raised several steps and could appear at the middle of the nave or on either side. It served as the place for the reading of the Scriptures and the Psalms or chants interspersed between the lessons; but at first the ambo was not for preaching. While functionally closer to our lectern, in design it is hardly distinguishable from a pulpit. Sometimes there might be more than one ambo, as in St. Clement's, Rome, one being used for Old Testament and Epistle readings and the other for the Gospel.

The space directly in front of the altar-table was often occupied by the lesser clergy or singers. A screen separated it from the rest of the nave, where the congregation stood. Seating for the whole congregation did not become common in some countries until the fourteenth century, and was never adopted in others. It is interesting to note that the men and women were carefully separated, even to restricting the women, in some cases, to galleries over the aisles. Since there was no seating, the congregation was free to move about and to crowd as close as possible to the liturgical center in use at any given moment. In most cases the baptismal font was in a separate building, the form of which will be discussed later.

The basilicas differed from each other in various ways, but in general were of the form described. They had the advantage of making each act of worship clearly visible to the congregation. Never did the chief clergy come between a liturgical center and the congregation. Congregation and clergy surrounded these centers instead, and yet the liturgical spaces allowed both groups to perform their functions in the liturgy without interfering in each other's work. The basilican arrangement combines the central pulpit (the bishop's throne) and the central altar-table. Both receive due emphasis without competing for attention and the two halves of worship (Word and sacrament) are given adequate expression.

<h1 style="text-align:center">III</h1>

As has been indicated, the best preserved pre-Constantinian church (Dura-Europos) clearly shows that different services of worship (baptism and eucharist) had distinct rooms provided for them. Thus from the earliest times of which we have clear information, specialized functions received distinct liturgical space, a fact too often obscured in the one-room church of today. As soon as the Church could safely erect buildings, different liturgical and devotional functions were provided for by distinct structures or by the divisions in one large building complex.

Two types of buildings were of special significance for later church building. These were the *martyrium*, the chapel over the grave or relics of a martyr, and the baptistery.

The *martyria* reflect the esteem for the relics of martyrs characteristic of the early Church. Often they were built upon the spot where the martyr had suffered and been buried. They were also erected at sites cherished for their significance in the life of Jesus, particularly in Bethlehem and Jerusalem. The *martyria* as separate buildings were more common in the East than the West. Architecturally, they reflected the influence of the tombs of wealthy families. This type of building was quite different from the basilica, which was organized around a horizontal axis. The *martyria* were buildings of a central type, the main axis being vertical. There was no sense of progression from one end to another, the tomb was in the center and an ambulatory (passage) encircled this central point.

Very similar in some respects was the baptistery, often a separate building in the early Church. Hundreds of these distinct baptisteries are known, including the famous ones at Florence, Ravenna, and Pisa. It is not by accident that the baptistery bore resemblances to the *martyria*. Though baptism at earliest times seems to have been administered in rivers, special buildings for it appear soon after the Peace of the Church. Square-shaped buildings seem to have been favored in the East, while circular, hexagonal, or octagonal buildings predominated in the West. In both cases, there was a clear parallel with the tombs of the vicinity.[10] Evidently this was deliberate, for death and resurrection were central concepts in the thought of the Church of this time regarding baptism. In baptism the believer was buried, lay dead, and was raised with Christ (Romans 6:3–4). Hence the font was often sunken in the center of the floor, the spot occupied in a *martyrium* by the principal tomb. It might be shaped as a cross, be circular to suggest the womb of rebirth, or octagonal to represent the resurrection (Easter being the first or eighth day of the week). Usually the font consisted of a tank or pool into which the candidate descended and from which he rose by means of steps. Most likely baptism was administered by having the candidate stand in the water and dip his head into it or by having water poured over his head (as dust and ashes were cast upon a corpse).[11] Even when pedestal fonts came into use they were sometimes recessed in the floor level so that the candidate descended into the grave (symbolically) and then rose in new life.

[10] J. G. Davies, *The Architectural Setting of Baptism* (London: Barrie and Rockliff, 1962), describes these and subsequent developments in detail. Excellent illustrations of fonts both ancient and modern appear in this book.

[11] Ibid. p. 26.

The baptisteries often included additional rooms in which other functions of the baptismal rite, such as robing, profession of faith, and anointing, might take place. The rite in early times involved a complex of actions, including what is now referred to as confirmation or reception into membership.[12] The baptisteries could accommodate a considerable number of candidates for baptism at one time, as at Florence.

It should be noted that both the *martyrium* and the baptistery are central buildings with the tomb or font in the center. Frequently the architectural focus matched this with a dome. The central type of building was to be a very influential one for the future of Christian worship, particularly in the Eastern Church and in Protestantism. Historically, this came about in the East through a complex of developments, particularly through the cult of relics after they were moved to parish churches. The influence of the *martyria* plus the development of new techniques in building domes over squares led to the gradual adoption of centralized buildings among Eastern Christians. In effect the basilican plan was combined with the central type of building in the East. The building type that became normative among the Byzantines was the dome over a square building, a style still favored among Orthodox Christians in the buildings they erect in the United States. Various other shapes could also be used, especially the Greek cross (a cross shape with equal arms), an octagon, or a square with one or three (prothesis, altar-table, relics) apses (Figure 3).

By and large the Orthodox churches have retained the tradition of the single altar-table, a practice different from that which developed in the West. Although early altar-tables were simple

---

[12] Cf. *The Apostolic Tradition of Hippolytus* translated and edited by Burton Scott Easton (New Haven: Archon, 1962), pp. 41–9. This early third-century treatise gives details on the baptismal service of the early Church and is one of the most significant documents for the early history of Christian worship.

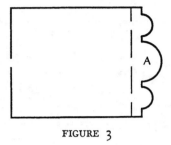

FIGURE 3

affairs, often made of wood, their dignity was sometimes stressed by placing a canopy above them. Gradually the sense developed in the Eastern Church of the eucharist as full of awe, dread, and mystery so great that the layman had to be shielded from it. Dix traces this tendency largely to the churches in Syria in the fourth century, whence emanated many influential concepts and practices in worship. Eventually the altar-table was placed behind a veil which could be drawn at moments in the liturgy to protect the laity from the holy mysteries within. In time a solid screen, the *iconostasis*, was added to the veil. This screen cut the church into two compartments, one for the laity and another for the clergy and the altar-table. The screen was pierced by three doors which could be opened at various times during the liturgy, but in effect the Eastern liturgies had become two services: that of the celebrant performing the most important actions inside the screen; and that of the people, led by a deacon, taking place outside the screen.

In Orthodox churches the exterior of the screen was covered with paintings of the saints. Indeed the walls and vaults of the church might be filled with representations in mosaics or murals of the saints. In one sense these fill a devotional function, for individual members of the congregation are apt to offer their own prayers before a favorite icon (image of a saint). Yet in Orthodox churches these images have a profound liturgical significance, for the common worship of Orthodox Christians is conceived of as

acts performed in heaven in eternity. Thus the worshipers stand
in the midst of the saints as all worship about the throne of the
heavenly Father. In churches of the Eastern Christians the saints
stand motionless in heavenly ecstasy rather than in one activity
or another as usual in Western representations. In the East the
icons stress the corporateness of the common worship of the
Church in heaven and on earth, a function which differs from
their usual use for personal devotions in the West.

IV

We turn our attention now to medieval developments in western
Europe. For two reasons this period is one of greatest importance
in understanding Protestant liturgical architecture. First of all,
late medieval architecture provided the point of departure for
Protestant church building in the Reformation, as the reformers
inherited both a building tradition and also thousands of medieval churches. Secondly, the nineteenth and twentieth centuries
have seen a major revival of medieval church architecture among
almost all Protestant bodies.

The course of the Middle Ages saw profound changes in the
manner in which worship was understood and conducted in the
West. In 1547, Stephen Gardiner, Bishop of Winchester, wrote a
long letter to Archbishop Cranmer in which he commented:

For in times past, when men came to church more diligently than
some do now, the people in the church took small heed what the
priest and the clerks did in the chancel, but only to stand up at the
Gospel and kneel at the Sacring [bell], or else every man was occupied him self severally [individually] in several prayer. And as for
the priests' prayer, they could not all have heard and understanded,
although they would, and had given ear thereunto. For such an enter-
prise to bring that to pass is impossible, without the priest should turn
his face to the people when he prays, and occupy many prayers to
them to make them hold their peace. And therefore it was never
meant that the people should indeed hear the Matins or hear the Mass,
but be present there and pray themselves in silence; with common

credit to the priests and clerks, that although they hear not a distinct sound to know what they say, yet to judge that they for their part were and be well occupied, and in prayer; and so should they be.[13]

Behind Bishop Gardiner's uncritical acceptance of the practice of "times past" lies a very profound change from the early Church's understanding of the laity's role in common worship. In his statement that the laity "took small heed" of what the clergy did during services, a statement which seems trustworthy, Gardiner is simply echoing the circumstances of the late Middle Ages. If the people could neither hear nor understand the services it is not strange that they did not take an active part in the mass aside from standing at the reading of the Gospel and gazing at the elevation. Clearly the people had lost their active roles in the public worship of the Church, becoming deaf and mute spectators. The doing of common worship had been largely monopolized by "the priest and the clerks."

On the other hand, Gardiner by no means assumes that the laity are idle. Far from that, they are engaged in personal devotions, every man being "occupied him self severally in several prayer." The time of public worship is spent in private prayer. Undoubtedly Gardiner could have cited other devotions, the telling of the rosary, the use of devotional treatises on the mass, and other popular practices. It is significant that these devotions had come to take precedence over an active participation in the mass or matins. Excluded from an active part in the liturgy, the laity had become involved in a variety of personal devotions conducted while the mass was being said by the priest.

The medieval period had seen a separation between the people and their clergy when it came to worship. In effect, the mass had become something which the clergy performed for the people, while the choir offices had likewise ceased to be the concern of the people. Father Jungmann notes of the medieval mass:

[13] *The Letters of Stephen Gardiner*, edited by James A. Muller (New York: Macmillan, 1933), p. 355. Spelling modernized.

The priest alone is active. The faithful, viewing what he is performing, are like spectators looking on at a mystery-filled drama of our
Lord's Way of the Cross. It is no accident, then, that Calderón in his
autos sacramentales should employ the traditional medieval allegory
to present a drama in which the whole economy of salvation, from
Paradise to world's end, is hinged to the Mass; and yet never a word,
either at the offertory or at the Communion, of the concelebration of
the laity.[14]

The clergy had become the professionals in common worship.
Gregory Dix characterizes the Western low mass "dialogued in
an undertone between priest and server" as a "degenerate . . .
representative of the old corporate worship of the eucharist," the
laity being "left with no active part in the rite at all." [15]

Such a situation did not come about overnight. Like most profound changes in worship, the role of the laity had disappeared
by a slow process of attrition. The fourth century had seen the
beginning of the quiescence of the laity in worship as the original
intimacy and discipline of the persecuted community was over-
whelmed by hordes of converts. A series of developments served
further to reduce the laity to a passive role. As northern Europe
was Christianized the Church was filled with people to whom
Latin was a strange tongue, yet the worship of the Church continued to be conducted in the language of the Romans. Increasingly the clergy and those in religious orders assumed the complete actions of worship.

Symptomatic of what was happening was the change in the
place of the altar-table. As we have seen in the fourth-century
basilica, the celebrant stood facing the people across the altar-
table, which itself might be located in the midst of the nave.
Gradually it became common in the West for the celebrant to

---

[14] Joseph A. Jungmann, S.J., *The Mass of the Roman Rite: Its Origins and
Developments,* translated by Francis A. Brunner, C.SS.R. (New York:
Benziger Brothers, 1951), I, 117.

[15] *The Shape of the Liturgy,* p. 484.

adopt a position between the people and the altar-table, a practice which predominated (outside Rome) by about A.D. 1000. The altar-table too was moved, gradually being pushed to the rear wall of the apse as far as possible from the congregation. No longer a free-standing table, it soon acquired a ledge and often a magnificent reredos (carved ornamental screen) behind it. With the priest standing between them and the altar-table and separated by the distance of a long chancel, the people became far removed from the chief liturgical center of the church.

Increasingly the mass itself became the subject of various allegorical interpretations. Though the laity took little direct part in the mass, they still were able to see much of it as it was celebrated by the priest. The allegorical significances taught in medieval manuals often had little if any direct relationship to the purpose of actions in the mass or furnishings in the building. So developed had these allegorical references become by the thirteenth century that William Durandus, Bishop of Mende, could give a detailed allegorical explanation of every item in the church building from the tiles on the roof (soldiers guarding the Church) to the steps to the altar-table (apostles and martyrs). His book, the *Rationale Divinorum Officiorum,* "constructed entirely on the basis of allegory, continued to be the liturgical handbook for the late Middle Ages and beyond." [16] Indeed it had abundant influence on the building of Protestant churches in the nineteenth century. Allegorical interpretations gave the people a subjective interpretation of the mass and the church building. Very frequently such symbolic thought completely obscured the actual purpose of actions of the mass or parts of the edifice.

In a somewhat similar vein, the Middle Ages saw the proliferation of various devotions in which the laity could engage during the mass or at other times. In many cases this involved devotional art, that is, objects with no direct relationship with the actual

[16] Jungmann, *The Mass of the Roman Rite* . . . , I, 115.

performance of the liturgy, which could be centers of personal devotions. Thus the laity, though deprived of access to some of the most important liturgical centers, were surrounded by a variety of devotional centers, each contributing to the offering of personal devotions.

V

We have seen that the early church allotted separate space for different liturgical functions. As early as the third century at Dura-Europos, baptism and the eucharist occur in separate rooms. This specialized use of space became even more pronounced in the Middle Ages, especially as the forms and types of worship became more complex. Not only do we see definite distinctions within a single building of the use of liturgical spaces, we see separate buildings reflecting different functions. It was the failure to notice the different purposes of each type of building that led the nineteenth-century gothic revival to some profound misunderstandings. It is important to examine some of these classifications briefly.

Certainly one of the most important types of church buildings in the Middle Ages were the churches erected for the use of monastic orders (Figure 4). The primary function of these build-

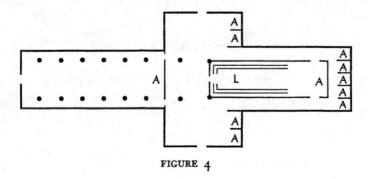

FIGURE 4

ings was to provide a setting for the daily offices, the seven hours and the night office which the monastic community recited as their work of God. The chief requisite for the offices was the choir stalls (hence the name choir offices), usually arranged along two parallel walls. This arrangement made it possible to sing hymns antiphonally. Often a lectern stood in the middle of the choir and the lessons would be read from it. The mass was also celebrated frequently, if not daily, in the religious houses, and the eastern end of the choir (the presbytery) would be reserved for the seating of those of the monastics who might be ordained. Immediately beyond them would appear the high altar and its accessories. The most important part of the monastic church, then, was the choir. The nave might be used on special occasions or, if it also served a parish church, frequently. But the choir was used several times daily and was a church within the church.

Often a screen was erected around the front and sides of the choir to keep out drafts, a matter of convenience in the vast un-heated churches, especially during the saying of the night office (at 2 a.m. in many houses). Far from intending to shut out wor-shipers, the screens were meant to enclose the members of the order, the customary congregations in these buildings. Frequently the screens in monastic churches were solid stone or wood, pierced only by a door into the nave. This typifies the prevalent medieval practice of dividing the church building up into a series of separate rooms according to function. Gradually the chancel assumed grandiose proportions, reflecting its importance and constant use. Beyond it would be the nave, occupied on occasion by laity not belonging to the order, and used for processions. Subsidiary altar-tables might be placed throughout the building so priests could say private masses.

Churches served by a group of clergy and known as collegiate churches developed along a similar pattern. Some of these, as well as monastic houses, came to be academic centers and a number developed a type of chapel in which the main portion of the building is the choir with a small western transept (arm) or ante-chapel. The stalls in the choir ran parallel to the long walls, with special stalls parallel to the screen between the choir and the ante-chapel. This pattern, known as the collegiate arrangement, was copied in some American seminary chapels and is common at the Oxford and Cambridge colleges in various forms. The members of the community occupied the stalls, whereas others found a place in the ante-chapel.

Another very significant building type was that evolved in the great cathedrals (Figure 5). The cathedral was distinguished

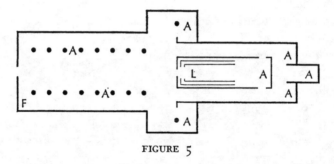

FIGURE 5

from other churches since it contained the bishop's throne and was thus the mother church of the whole diocese. Its function was not that of a parish church, though various congregations might use the building or those adjacent to it. In many cases the cathedrals were staffed by monastic communities; but even when staffed by secular clergy they often had a magnificent choir set aside for the use of the resident body. In the cathedrals the clergy and singers provided the usual body of worshipers, and the choir arrangement was the best possible for their worship since on most occasions no other worshipers would be present. This arrangement came to have great consequences:

The idea of a choir cut off from the nave for the exclusive use of the clergy was copied by thirteenth- and fourteenth-century bishops in building cathedrals for secular canons. Their cathedrals became models for parish churches; and it thus came about that a type of church, planned to separate first monastic communities, and then secular canons, from the laity, eventually succeeded in determining the arrangement of our parish churches, and separating the clergy from their people in the liturgy.[17]

Other arrangements besides the eastern choir were also known. In Germany a western apse might contain the choir stalls, and in Spain space in the middle of the nave might be walled in for the choir.

But the typical medieval cathedral was far more complex than two rooms. Indeed it was often conceived of as a series of rooms, each serving a particular purpose and separated from the others by walls or screens. Many of these screens were removed in the last two centuries with the purpose of creating vistas, but the original builders were more concerned with functions than awesome views. Some of the great cathedrals and monastic churches treasured relics of popular saints and became the object of pilgrimages. Space had to be provided for the shrine, often located behind the high altar, and for processions to and from the shrine. Various chapels were added for particular devotions, especially those of the Virgin Mary. Sections of the cathedrals in the late Middle Ages were screened off for chantry chapels, in which wealthy persons and clergy were buried and altars erected in order that mass could be said for the repose of their souls. In the fourteenth and fifteenth centuries such chapels became common in monastic, cathedral, collegiate, and parish churches. In towns, trade guilds often collaborated to build such chapels. Often chantry chapels consisted of a section of the nave or chancel aisle partitioned off, but they could also be an extension of the building itself. Thus the interior space of the medieval cathedral was broken up into a series of rooms, each having a specific function.

[17] G. W. O. Addleshaw and Frederick Etchells, *The Architectural Setting of Anglican Worship* (London: Faber and Faber, 1948), p. 17.

During the Middle Ages a number of churches were erected by the Franciscan and Dominican orders, primarily as preaching churches. These diverged somewhat from the usual parish church building, as they were designed as large well-lighted halls to be used for preaching and were really ancillary to the parish church.

The erection of baptisteries as separate buildings continued in the Middle Ages as late as the fourteenth century, though most of these were in southern Europe. They commonly repeated the forms of the baptisteries of the early Church, though increasingly fonts found a location inside the parish church.

VI

By far the most important church building for the average man in the Middle Ages was his parish church. Not only did it provide the place where he attended mass, but it was where he heard sermons, practiced his devotions, saw drama, conducted much of his social and business life, and after this life he might be buried beneath the floor, confidently expecting to be inside the familiar walls when raised from the dead at the last judgment.

Like the other types of churches of the period, the late medieval parish church had developed into a complex of spaces divided by screens. Developing from a rather simple two-cell building in the early Middle Ages, the parish church by the fifteenth century had become a very complex structure.[18] To the original nave and small chancel had been added, in many cases, aisles, chapels, a porch or two, and a tower (Figure 6). The chancel had been extended so that it might be half or two-thirds as long as the nave. Quite likely the roof of the nave had been raised to admit clerestory windows over the aisles.

[18] For surveys of these developments see A. H. Thompson, *The Historical Growth of the English Parish Church* (Cambridge: University Press, 1911) and *The Ground Plan of the English Parish Church* (Cambridge: University Press, 1911).

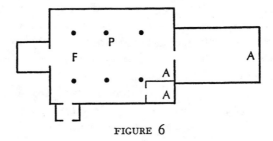

FIGURE 6

The main division in the building remained that between the chancel and the nave. Indeed, in Church law the two portions were virtually treated as separate buildings, the clergy or lay rector being responsible for the upkeep of the chancel and the churchwardens charged with the maintenance of the church proper (nave). The chancel provided the space for worship by the clergy, including both the saying of the mass and the recital of the daily offices. Frequently the lord of the manor and his family occupied stalls in the chancel, but otherwise the laity were generally excluded. The nave, on the other hand, was allotted to the laity. From here they could glimpse the mass offered on their behalf in the chancel, though occasionally it might be offered at an altar-table in the nave. Here were the pulpit and the font; and here the layman was surrounded by a vast array of paintings, statues, and images meant to instruct him and to stimulate his devotions.

The division between the chancel and the nave was the rood screen, so named because of the large cross (rood) that surmounted it. Whereas the screens in monastic and cathedral churches were usually solid barriers, those in parish churches were often made of wooden tracery that allowed the laity a glimpse of all that went on in the chancel. In the conventual and cathedral churches the screen enclosed the usual congregation (the residential bodies); in the parish church the screen divided the congregation (the laity) from the clergy. Occasionally, above the screen was a choir loft, and sometimes an organ. The most obvious feature above the screen was the crucifix, with figures of Mary and John gazing up at it. The screen divided the chancel (for worship by the clergy) from the nave (for worship by the people) yet did not completely isolate either group.

The late medieval parish church was likely to include one or more chapels, either those dedicated to various saints or chantries where masses could be said for the repose of the souls of deceased persons. These might be actually located in the nave and its aisles, in which case they were separated from the main space by parclose screens. Increasingly, additional altar-tables were added to the church and even small parish churches might have several in the nave in addition to that in the chancel. Occasionally transepts were added, making a cruciform church, and the eastern walls of these were provided with altar-tables. Other lateral extensions provided space for chantries and other chapels.

The porch of the medieval church had two important liturgical functions: it was the scene of a major portion of the marriage ceremony and also the location of part of the baptismal service. Directly outside was usually the churchyard, entered by means of the lych gate at which the priest met the corpse during the burial services. The porch also provided a spot for ratifying business contracts "at church door," and above it there might be a schoolroom or guildhall.

Every portion of the medieval church was arranged according to its liturgical or devotional function. It should be borne in mind that the basic plan was that of a longitudinal church, though this might be obscured by lateral extensions. Basically, the building consisted of a rectangle occupied by the laity and another rectangle for the clergy. The hierarchical distinction between the laity and the clergy was unmistakable, as the clergy had access to the holiest spot in the building, the high altar, which most of the laity rarely, if ever, approached.

The liturgical centers of the parish church were likewise significant, both by reason of their design and their location.[19] The chancel included most of these centers. Against the east wall was the high altar, the visual center of the chancel if not of the whole building. Behind it there might be a carved reredos. Candles began to appear on it after 1100, and the crucifix on the altar-table probably in the thirteenth century. Solid stone altars became the rule after about a thousand years of wooden altar-tables. The stone altar enclosed relics of saints and reinforced the idea of sacrifice. There were other fixtures about the altar-table used for the reserved sacrament, as well as the piscina, used for the washing of the vessels, and the sedilia where the celebrants sat. Altar rails do not seem to have become common until the sixteenth century. At the other end of the chancel were the stalls for the clergy and the lord of the manor's family. In the midst of the choir might appear a lectern to be used in the choir offices.

The nave usually contained several altar-tables, traditionally against an eastern wall and used for various private masses. One or more might stand against the screen and be used on the rare occasions when the laity received communion. The pulpit was in the nave, often along one of the piers halfway down one side of the nave. Medieval pulpits were often magnificent stone or wooden structures, usually beautifully carved. At the west end of the nave near one of the entrances was the font. The prevalent practice in the Middle Ages was the baptism of infants by submersion. Most often the fonts were of stone with a bowl about two feet across and a foot deep, and usually protected with a cover which could be locked to prevent the theft of holy water.[20] The position near the door was symbolic of entrance into the Church and perhaps a survival of the position of the catechumens in the ancient Church. The main space of the nave was

[19] Cf. illustrations of these in Francis Bond, *The Chancel of English Churches* (London: Oxford University Press, 1916), and other volumes of the *Church Art in England* series.

[20] Cf. J. G. Davies, *The Architectural Setting of Baptism*, Ch. II.

allotted to the laity who stood or knelt for the service. Fixed seating was a late development in Western churches, not becoming common in some areas before the fourteenth century. With its introduction the laity became irretrievably stationary. The comfort thus gained by the laity sitting down on the job was obtained at the price of rigidity of location and has ever since tended to discourage congregational processions and attention to liturgical centers other than those directly in front of the people. The liturgical space occupied by the congregation has ever since been conceived of in rigid terms instead of as a space in which the laity can move about.

Of greatest importance to the average man of the Middle Ages were the devotional centers of his church. The most obvious of these was the rood, which dominated the nave. Here the worshiper in the nave could contemplate the scene of Calvary in life-size representation. Inside the chancel the crucifix upon the high altar provided a similar focus for the clergy's devotions. The cult of the passion was further carried out in the fourteen stations of the cross arranged around the nave.

Very common in medieval parish churches were paintings of the last judgment, which often occupied the wall above the chancel arch. Here the faithful could contemplate the bliss of the good and the tortures of the wicked. The cults of the saints were encouraged by placing figures, painted, carved, and glazed, about the building. Indeed there must have been very little barren space in the medieval church. The reserved sacrament was also the center of an extra-liturgical devotion. Hung over an altar-table in a pyx, locked in a cupboard (aumbry), or enshrined in a sacrament house, the consecrated bread was understood to be the real physical presence of Christ. In later times it was placed in a monstrance where it was visible and could be exposed and adored.

Precisely because common worship had become so completely professionalized, the layman of the Middle Ages turned to personal devotions, and his part of the church building was amply supplied with devotional centers. These so-called extra-liturgical decorations in the nave have been the subject of criticism recently. Father H. A. Reinhold writes:

Should the place for these decorations not be in devotional chapels, on the pulpit, or in the vestibule, instead of the sanctuary, or the nave of the church, which is so definitely focused on the mystery of the altar, so much more comprehensive and wide than these "excisions," these partial or angular aspects? Is the meditative, historical and discursive method of the Rosary and the Stations not on a different level, different from the "Sacramental re-presentation, not merely mental, but of symbolic reality," of the Eucharist? Should they then be in the nave? Not rather in chapels? [21]

For the modern Protestant these questions are not as irrelevant as they might seem. For the medieval Catholic there was little choice. Excluded from an active role in the liturgy, he quite naturally turned to cultivating his devotional life, using the nave of his church as the place, and the time of mass as the most convenient occasion.

[21] *Speaking of Liturgical Architecture* (Notre Dame: Liturgical Programs, University of Notre Dame, 1952), p. 25. This is an excellent booklet, well worth being read by Protestants.

IV

Reformation Experiments

The work of the Protestant reformers of the sixteenth century cannot be understood apart from the conditions of the late Middle Ages. Although the reformers condemned, with varying degrees of harshness, the practices of contemporary Catholicism, they themselves were nevertheless the products of this tradition. Many of the reformers had been priests and members of religious orders; all had worshiped and received their education with fellow Catholics. Thus even when they criticized abuses, their very language and thought patterns were conditioned by medieval Catholicism.

Very few generalizations can safely be made about the reformers of the sixteenth century but it is almost axiomatic that the hope of these men was to recover the doctrine and practices of the Church of the New Testament and first centuries. Calvin's *The Form of Church Prayers* (1542) proclaimed itself to be *According to the Custom of the Ancient Church*. The reformers disagreed on how much tradition since the early Church was innocent and agreeable, but they concurred on the importance of return to the biblical sources.

Yet, as the Reformation showed full well, return to any other period in time is impossible. In the first place, the reformers knew much less about the worship of the first three centuries than they thought they did, or, for that matter, than we think we do. Despite all efforts to make it such, the New Testament was never intended to be a liturgical handbook. Furthermore, the reformers could not detach themselves from the thought patterns of their place in time and space. The passion of Christ tended to dominate their approach to worship as it had western Christendom for several centuries. Their congregations were as susceptible to individualism in worship as their medieval ancestors. The very theological terms the reformers used had given birth to concepts they now rejected. Even if the reformers had been able to free themselves from the practices of their time and culture, they would have found it difficult to impose such a radical break upon their people. Calvin found it impossible to impose weekly communion on those for whom yearly communion had been a norm, no matter how common such a practice had been in the early Church.

Having said this much, it must be remembered that the reformers did succeed in approximating many items of primitive practice, especially in worship. Indeed so much was at stake in the Reformation era that it is easy to overlook the fact that this was a time of tremendous liturgical renewal, an element linking the sixteenth century and our own time.

One of the most striking keynotes of the Reformation was the attempt to recover a concept of the Church as consisting of the whole body of Christ, both lay and clerical, a fact which the clericalism of the late Middle Ages had tended to obscure in worship. The reformers emphasized that the laity in their daily work are engaged in the service of God through the social nature of their work as much as the clergy in their daily tasks. As Luther put it, all workers can serve God as much as the priest.[1] If the

[1] "An Open Letter to the Christian Nobility of the German Nation," *Works of Martin Luther* (Philadelphia ed.; Philadelphia: Muhlenberg, 1943), II, 69.

layman served God through his vocation, then certainly he should be allowed to offer his work of worship in the Church service in his own priestly role. Thus every layman is a priest with his own liturgy, his own proper work to do in common worship.

In order to make this possible, the reformers were almost unanimous in agreeing that the services should be said in a language "understanded of the people." Furthermore, the service should be conducted in such a manner that the people could hear distinctly the words of the minister. Even this was not enough, for most of the reformers insisted that all acts of the service be made visible to the congregation. Some had the services printed in books so the people could also read the prayers with their minister. In the Lutheran and other traditions hymn singing became an important part of the congregation's work of worship.

The Reformation was marked by efforts to restore the primitive balance between the service centering on Scripture and preaching with that of the eucharist. In many traditions the recovery of preaching as worship was extremely successful. The reformers were less successful in the retention of the eucharist as the other half of Christian worship. It was not until the advent of Methodism in the eighteenth century that the practice of frequent communion was actually achieved in a popular movement and then it lasted only briefly.

These changes had a profound impact on Protestant liturgical architecture. The experiments attempted in the sixteenth century and the two centuries that followed were so varied and rich that it is possible to consider only a limited number of them. But it is very important that we be aware of the possibilities that they offer. Some of them have been rediscovered in our own time as possibilities to be explored, and even those which we must reject are not without interest. The remainder of this chapter will be a sampling of some of these experiments.

I

In the sixteenth century the most immediate architectural problem facing the reformers was not the design of new churches but the transformation of the medieval churches they had inherited into forms suitable for Protestant worship. This provided problems to task their ingenuity and it is interesting to see the various solutions they found. In most areas the medieval Church left an abundance of buildings and it was not until war or fire destroyed many of them that Protestants were forced to create their own building types. Thousands of these medieval buildings survive even today, something like nine thousand in Great Britain alone. The sixteenth century saw a series of adaptations of medieval buildings. In some cases these are instructive for modern congregations confronted with the problems of a gothic revival building.

The Lutherans in Germany and elsewhere tended to be rather conservative in their treatment of medieval buildings. Luther had prevented Carlstadt from carrying out a thorough iconoclasm in 1522. He was inclined toward conceding freedom in the retention of images, vestments, candles, and solid altars, having an appreciation of ecclesiastical art not shared by all the reformers. Luther's preference was having the celebrant stand behind the altar-table, facing the congregation. By and large the medieval arrangements persisted in Lutheran churches, font and altar-table retaining their original places.[2] Other groups were less conservative. In the Grosse Kirche (Reformed) in Emden the chancel was turned into a room for the Lord's supper with a table reaching down its length. A chapel was set aside for weddings and other services were performed in the nave.

[2] Cf. Vereinigung Berliner Architekten, *Der Kirchenbau des Protestantismus von der Reformation bis zur Gegenwart* (Berlin: Kommissions-Verlag von Ernst Toeche, 1893).

Experiments in the Netherlands, where the Reformed tradition was dominant, were more radical than among the Lutherans.[3] In many cases the chancel was abandoned altogether for purposes of worship. Even today in the Netherlands some ancient chancels serve only as tombs for admirals or for the parking of bicycles. The paintings of a seventeenth-century artist, Pieter Saenredam, show a number of medieval churches devoid of ornamentation. The chief liturgical center now has become the pulpit situated in the middle of one side of the nave, a position not distant from that which it had in the Middle Ages. The congregation then stood or sat in concentric circles about the pulpit. Frequently, the pulpits are huge with tremendous sounding boards overhead. Special seats were provided for the magistrates, and the woodwork and brass chandeliers were often beautifully designed and executed. Movable tables were erected when holy communion was celebrated.

In Scotland the Reformed tradition followed rather similar patterns.[4] The pulpit became the dominant liturgical center and it frequently stood in the center of one side of the nave. Occasionally, a lateral extension was made at right angles to the nave opposite the pulpit. Frequently, a bracket was placed on the pulpit to hold a basin for baptism. At communion time long tables were set up in the aisles, and the people received sitting around them. This practice persisted until the nineteenth century in Scotland and still exists in the Netherlands. Sometimes galleries were added at the ends of the building or opposite the pulpit to increase the accommodation. For economic reasons, large me-

[3] Cf. M. D. Ozinga, *De Protestantsche Kerkenbouw in Nederland* (Amsterdam: H. J. Paris, 1929); and *Protestantsche Kerkbouw*, edited by J. N. Bakhuizen van den Brink (Arnhem: S. Gouda Quint–D. Brouwer en Zoon, 1946).

[4] Cf. George Hay, *The Architecture of Scottish Post-Reformation Churches, 1560–1843* (Oxford: Clarendon Press, 1957); and Ian G. Lindsay, *The Scottish Parish Kirk* (Edinburgh: Saint Andrew Press, 1960).

dieval churches were occasionally divided by screens to serve several congregations.

English churchmen were generally more conservative in their treatment of medieval buildings. Reflecting Martin Bucer's belief that the minister should lead the service "from a position from which the things said may by all present be apprehended abundantly," [5] Anglican reformers were guided by the need to make the service audible and visible to their congregations. During the reign of King Edward VI (1547–53) many stone altars were demolished and replaced by movable wooden tables. The reasons for this were theological: Bishop Nicholas Ridley and others felt Christ had put an end to sacrifices and that the table was the primitive form. Accordingly "God's board" replaced the immovable stone altar. The Lord's table was set up in some "convenient" spot, a significant term since the emphasis is placed on function rather than on symbolism. In the time of Edward VI this convenient spot could include a table running the length of the chancel (tablewise) or parallel but detached from the east wall (altarwise). In these positions the communicants could kneel on all sides of the "Lord's Table," an arrangement increasingly sought today. Quite frequently the altar-table was moved into the nave, convenience again being the keynote.

Under Queen Elizabeth I the roods were destroyed but the screens were retained. Increasingly, reading desks were erected for the minister in the nave of the church from which the service might be read. Most of the medieval shrines and images had been destroyed under Edward VI, but the Elizabethans added the Ten Commandments painted on a board and these eventually were often accompanied by the Apostles' Creed and the Lord's Prayer. The basic arrangement of the medieval buildings adapted for Anglican worship often remained that of a two-room church; the chancel in which the communicants assembled at the words

[5] Cf. G. W. O. Addleshaw and Frederick Etchells, *The Architectural Setting of Anglican Worship* (London: Faber & Faber, 1948), p. 245.

"draw near," and the nave in which the other services were conducted. Thus the principle remained in effect of different rooms for different services, but in this case the laity were no longer barred from any portion of the church. Laity and clergy worshiped together in whichever room was in use at any given time. At communion both moved to the chancel; otherwise, both remained in the nave.

II

The sixteenth century was a time of adapting already existing buildings for Protestant worship and relatively few new structures were built. This situation was to change in the seventeenth century by the destruction of multitudes of old buildings by war and fire, and in some areas the need for new buildings for various denominations arose, cities grew, and new areas were settled. The seventeenth century is a fascinating time, for in it the various denominations achieved distinctive buildings designed especially for their particular purposes. In the eighteenth century further experiments were carried out though often these were elaborations and refinements of the basic conceptions about Protestant church building worked out in the seventeenth century. One cannot fail to be impressed by the immense variety of experiments carried out by Protestants in the seventeenth and eighteenth centuries. Some of these may suggest points of departure for contemporary church architecture. All that can be given here is a sampling, but it is intended to suggest the richness of this heritage.[6]

In general it can be said that German Protestants showed both a strong conservatism and yet a willingness to experiment in the churches they built in the seventeenth and eighteenth centuries.

[6] Cf. Anthony Garvan, "The Protestant Plain Style before 1630," *Journal of the Society of Architectural Historians*, IX (1950), 5–13. This article provides a good general survey of the period.

One sees a strong survival of the prominent altar-table, topped by a large crucifix, and frequently having a magnificent reredos. Not only did the altar-table and its accessories remain prominent but it was often accorded its own liturgical space in an area at the east end of the building not greatly distinct from a chancel except by the absence of a screen.

At the same time, there was a willingness to use a new architectural style, the baroque, which Lutherans used with as much enthusiasm as did Roman Catholics. To the Protestant, accustomed only to English or American Protestant architecture, the richness of Lutheran baroque in Germany and Scandinavia is amazing. No term can describe it so adequately as the word "dramatic." All manner of architectural devices were used to give dramatic emphasis to the chief liturgical centers of the buildings. The altar-tables were bathed with daylight from windows high overhead. Pulpits dazzle one with their gilt and carving.[7] Similar ornamentation was lavished on the organ cases, emphasizing the great use made of music in the Lutheran service. It should be remembered that such a wealth of color and carving often called attention to the main liturgical centers of the building as well as decorating the interior.

A frequent innovation in German churches was the introduction of galleries. Indeed in the course of time the gallery almost became the distinctive trademark of the Protestant church. Nowhere was it carried to such extremes as in Germany where successive rows of galleries were added, sometimes making five tiers. The result reminds one of an opera house. The purpose, of course, was to bring as many people near to the pulpit as possible. This usually necessitated high pulpits, often placed at the second-story level. Usually the galleries were ranged on the wall opposite the pulpit, but often followed the shape of the interior to surround the pulpit. The conditions for preaching were thus

[7] Cf. Peter Poscharsky, "Kurze Entwicklungsgeschichte der Kanzel," *Kunst und Kirche*, II (1960).

excellent, but such buildings can be regarded as symptoms of the decline of frequent communion, such an act being difficult with galleries unless (as with the Puritans) communion were served in the pews. Galleries also caused certain problems on the exterior since they cut across windows.

In many German churches there evolved a desire to bring the principal liturgical centers together as much as possible in the so-called *prinzipalstück*. Frequently pulpit and altar-table were combined as in the village church of Sessen (built in 1707) where the pulpit is directly above the altar-table and forms a canopy over it. This arrangement was not uncommon, and in many instances the font was placed directly before the altar-table and the organ case immediately above the pulpit.

In many churches conservatism retained the longitudinal medieval arrangement with the altar-table at the end of a long nave or in a structural chancel. Examples appear in the Marienkirche in Wolfenbüttel (1608–23), the village church at Nidda (1615–18), the Stadtkirche in Bückeburg (1615), or in the Katharinen-Kirche in Frankfort on the Main (1678–80).[8] But there was a great number of experiments with new shapes. One of the earliest of these, the church at Freudenstadt (1601–8), is L-shaped, the free-standing altar-table appearing at the juncture of the arms together with the font, pulpit and organ (Figure 7). There are galleries at the extremities of the arms. Thus a fairly large number of people are brought close to the liturgical centers, but the congregation is divided into two quite distinct groups, probably men and women in this case.

Other experiments followed. A T-form church had some popularity in the eighteenth century. In this the congregation sat on three sides of the liturgical centers which appeared at the junction of the arms. Such an arrangement was in the former Petrikirche in Berlin (1730–33) and the Marienkirche in Grossenhain

[8] Cf. *Der Kirchenbau des Protestantismus* for illustrations of many of these buildings.

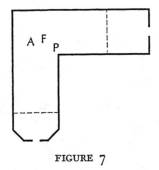

FIGURE 7

(1748). In the latter building the pulpit is above and behind the altar-table at the level of the second (middle) gallery (Figure 8).

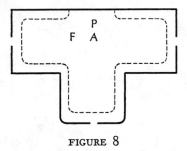

FIGURE 8

A fairly common form was the cross church which could vary from the Greek cross with equal arms to a Latin cross with a long nave. In cross churches the altar-table might appear in a small chancel with the pulpit at the crossing (Gnadenkirche in Hirschberg, 1709–18), the pulpit and altar both in one transept (church in Schmiedeberg, 1713–16), or both pulpit and altar at the crossing as in the Jerusalem-Kirche in Berlin, 1726–28 (Figure 9).

Polygonal and round churches had considerable popularity. These might include the liturgical centers at the juncture of two sides (Neue Kirche in the Gendarmen-Markt in Berlin, 1701–3), in the middle of a side (Church in Niendorf near Hamburg,

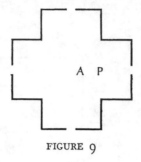

FIGURE 9

1775–80) or in a separate apse as in the famous Frauenkirche in Dresden, 1726–38 (Figure 10). This remarkable building with its five rows of galleries had a lectern at the front of the chancel, a font directly behind, and the altar-table at the rear of the chancel beneath an elaborate reredos with the organ towering above. The pulpit was at the juncture of the chancel and the central

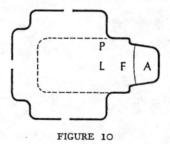

FIGURE 10

space. Round churches were also built (Dreifaltigkeits-Kirche in Berlin, 1737–39), and elliptical churches with the liturgical centers at a short end (church in Alten near Dessau, 1743), or at a broad side (Pauls-Kirche, Frankfort on the Main, 1787–1833).

The general tendency of these experiments was that of securing a central type church, a building in which there is a close sense of unity between the congregation and the liturgical centers. Thus the liturgical space occupied by the congregation merges readily with that used by the clergy. Every act is visible and the spoken word easily heard by the maximum number of people. Similar practices developed in other Protestant lands.

In the nearby Netherlands a different Protestant tradition was dominant, that of the Reformed churches, but the same type of search for appropriate forms continued. There were some real differences however from the Lutheran tradition. The Dutch tended to be more restrained in matters of ornamentation, though they lavished decoration on elaborate organ cases and built many fine pulpits, usually with large sounding boards. In Dutch Reformed churches the problem of design was somewhat different from Lutheran churches as the pulpit was the only liturgical center of importance. This meant that the problem which had perplexed German architects, how to make font, altar-table, and pulpit all prominent, was no difficulty. The altar-tables in Reformed churches in the Netherlands were (and in many instances have remained) portable furnishings which were set up when the Lord's supper was celebrated so that the congregation could sit around the altar-table. Thus long tables extended down the aisles or across the front of the church, but, since this would be an inconvenience except on the occasions when the sacrament was celebrated, they would be removed after communion. The font likewise was of minor visual significance. It might be only a basin placed in a hoop on the pulpit or put on a table when needed. Thus the pulpit was left the single dominant liturgical center of the building. With this simplification the chief problem was to accommodate the greatest number of people as close as possible to the pulpit so that all present could hear and see the minister as he led the congregation in worship.

Yet the variety of experiments conducted in providing the optimum shape is interesting. The oldest of these is the church at Willemstad, a perfect octagon (built 1596–1607).[9] The pulpit is in the center of one side and the rest of the building is filled with

[9] For illustrations and plans see Ozinga, *Protestantsche Kerken,* and Bakhuizen van den Brink, *Protestantsche Kerkbouw.*

pews. A very simple and direct solution, it appears in a more sophisticated form in the Mare Church in Leiden, 1649 (Figure 11) and the Oostkerk in Middleburg, 1667. Octagonal churches were erected by the Dutch in America but all have disappeared.[10] Perhaps even more important was John Wesley's adoption of the octagon for Methodist preaching-houses, most likely derived from Dutch prototypes.

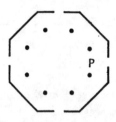

FIGURE 11

Another interesting variety appears in the "New" Church (1656) in the Hague. Basically the building is in the shape of a dumb-bell, the pulpit appearing in the very short crossarm (Figure 12). A somewhat similar arrangement can be seen in the

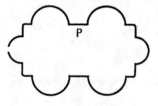

FIGURE 12

Westerkerk in Amsterdam (1630) where two sets of short transepts intersect a rectangular nave. Square buildings were tried as

[10] Hugh Morrison, *Early American Architecture from the First Colonial Settlements to the National Period* (New York: Oxford University Press, 1952), pp. 117–18.

in the New Church, Haarlem, 1649, and the Oosterkerk, Amsterdam, 1671 (Figure 13), the pulpit standing in the center of one
side but well out from the wall. Another pattern was the Greek
cross church which (as in the Noorder Kerk, Amsterdam, 1623)

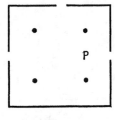

FIGURE 13

might have bevelled corners and the pulpit located in one corner
(Figure 14). The New Church in Emden (1647) was T-shaped
in its interior arrangement though the exterior resembled five-
eighths of an octagon. The emphasis in these churches is over-
whelmingly in the direction of a central type of building.

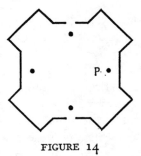

FIGURE 14

It is more difficult to trace patterns among French Protestants
since after the Revocation of the Edict of Nantes in 1685 the
churches (or temples as they were called) were destroyed. One
building, though, was to have considerable importance. This was

the famed temple of Charenton (Figure 15) built in 1623.[11] A large building, capable of holding between four and five thousand worshipers, it was basically a very simple rectangle with two rows of galleries on all four sides. About one quarter of the length of the nave from the east end stood the pulpit platform having seats for the ministers. No doubt the influence of this

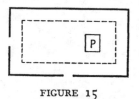

FIGURE 15

building was great in other lands, though there seems to have been a tendency to overestimate this. Charenton and other temples were destroyed in 1685. For much of the ensuing century French Protestants worshiped in secret, often gathered in woods and barns about a portable pulpit. In a sense these portable pulpits surrounded by worshipers represent the Reformed church building in microcosm.

In Scotland the same theological tradition was represented by the Presbyterian Church of Scotland. The liturgical essentials, as laid down by the 1560 *Book of Discipline*, were to include a pulpit, a baptismal basin, and tables for the Lord's supper. As in the Church of the Netherlands, the pulpit was the dominant center. Silver or pewter basins were often attached to it by brackets for baptism. Until the nineteenth century the people sat about long communion tables which were erected when needed.

The first Protestant Church built in Scotland is the 1592 parish church of Burntisland, a square building with a gallery, the pul-

11 Cf. "Le Temple de Charenton 1606–1685," *Bulletin de la Société de l'Histoire du Protestantisme Français*, V (1857), 173–8. Sir George Wheler described this building for Englishmen in 1689 in *An Account of the Churches or Places of Assembly of the Primitive Christians* (London: 1689), p. 117.

pit being against one of the central piers.[12] Rectangular churches, usually with the pulpit in the center of one long wall, were prevalent in the seventeenth century. In Scotland T-shaped churches seem to have had an unusual popularity. They were derived from rectangular buildings, the extra arm often accommodating a burial vault and the loft of the patron. Examples remain at Anstruther Easter (1636) or Ayr (1654) and the same type remained popular in the eighteenth century as at Reay, 1739 (Figure 16). Cruciform churches also had a popularity in Scot-

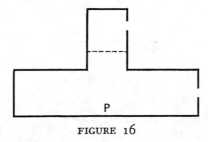

FIGURE 16

land, particularly Greek cross Fenwick (1643) and Lauder, 1673 (Figure 17). Octagons were tried also as at Kelso (1773) and

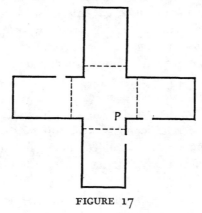

FIGURE 17

[12] Cf. Hay, *The Architecture of Scottish Post-Reformation Churches* for illustrations and plans.

Dreghorn, 1780 (Figure 18). In all of these experiments the dominant pattern was the central church with the people gathered as closely as possible about the pulpit.

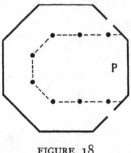

FIGURE 18

We see a rather different pattern emerging in the Anglican tradition in England. Although Calvinistic theology had a wide influence within the Church of England, considerable elements of Catholic tradition were retained or reasserted themselves in worship. Thus the altar-table remained a generally prominent liturgical furnishing in the seventeenth and eighteenth centuries though not necessarily used any more frequently than in the Reformed tradition. Very few churches were built in England prior to the 1660s though various parties had long struggled to control and rearrange the existing parish churches of the nation. During the 1640s and 50s the Puritan party controlled the nation's churches which were subjected to a further cleansing of popish relics. Actually the account of William Dowsing, a Puritan who recorded his iconoclasm in a *Journal*,[13] indicates that most of the more accessible objects that gave offense had long since been removed by Anglicans. After 1660 Puritans were re-

[13] *The Journal of William Dowsing* edited by C. H. E. White (Ipswich: Pawsey and Hayes, 1885).

pressed by a series of laws and it was not until 1689 that they were free to develop their own building type in England.[14]

The great landmark in Anglican church building is the work of Sir Christopher Wren (1632–1723). In 1666 a fire devastated a major portion of London, destroying eighty-four city churches. Wren was chosen as the architect for more than fifty of the buildings replacing those destroyed in the fire, and his work was a major influence on English church building for almost two hundred years. A large measure of the success of Wren's buildings as the setting for Anglican worship derives from his careful analysis of the function of the Protestant church building. He wrote of the necessity "in our reformed Religion . . . that all who are present can both hear and see." [15] In contrast with the churches of the Roman Catholics "ours are to be fitted for Auditories" thus enabling "all to hear the Service, and both to hear distinctly, and see the Preacher." Wren even computed how close a person had to be in front, behind, and beside the pulpit in order "to hear distinctly."

Wren was in a position to start afresh in the style of his building which he did by adopting the ancient Roman secular basilica as his point of departure, and combining it with staged towers, often strongly gothic in form if not in details. Subsequent versions became the prototype for the church towers of eighteenth-century American meetinghouses. But Wren was also subject to a tradition concerning the liturgical centers of a church. In the 1630s Archbishop Laud had brought about a return of the altar-table to its late medieval position against the east wall of the chancel. Laud had also succeeded in securing a practice of en-

---

14 Cf. an excellent article by John Betjeman, "Nonconformist Architecture," *Architectural Review*, LXXXVIII (1940), 161–74; also Martin S. Briggs, *Puritan Architecture and Its Future* (London: Lutterworth, 1946); Ronald P. Jones, *Nonconformist Church Architecture* (London: Lindsey Press, 1914).

15 *Parentalia* (London: 1750), p. 320.

closing the altar-tables with rails at which communicants knelt to receive communion.[16] Altar rails evidently had been introduced in Roman Catholic churches during the sixteenth century; they were superfluous in medieval churches with roodscreens but in screenless baroque Catholic churches and Anglican buildings they protected the altar-table and defined the liturgical space about it. It is questionable in the present day whether such protection (particularly against dogs) is necessary. Kneeling is certainly possible without rails though a change in floor level is a great convenience. The Laudian altar was frequently emphasized by a window behind or a reredos including the Ten Commandments which the canon laws of 1604 had ordered "be set up on the East end of every Church and Chapel."

The canons of 1604 further provided "that a convenient seat be made for the Minister to read service in" and that the churchwardens "shall provide a comely and decent Pulpit, to be set in a convenient place." In addition there was to be a "Font of stone . . . set in the ancient usual places." In Wren's time the reading desk ("convenient seat") had become the most important liturgical center, the whole service (except sermon) being conducted from this place except when communion was celebrated. Occasionally, the reading pew and pulpit were combined with a clerk's seat to form the three-decker pulpit. Its advantage was in dramatizing the essential unity of various acts of worship in a service by conducting them from one liturgical center.

Wren's great genius was in building churches organized around the liturgical principles which had emerged in over a century of worship according to the *Book of Common Prayer*. It may even be argued that the temporary use of former Puritan preaching halls during the rebuilding of the city churches influenced Wren's clients to insist upon buildings which took the demands

---

[16] Cf. Addleshaw and Etchells, *The Architectural Setting of Anglican Worship*, pp. 120–47.

of preaching seriously.[17] At any rate, Wren's churches succeeded in making it eminently possible for the congregation to take part in the liturgy as well as to hear the sermon within buildings which were of high esthetic order. Frequently Wren's churches were built on peculiarly shaped lots. The shapes of his buildings include a wide variety of polygons, rectangles, and trapezoids.[18] Basically they are one-room buildings. Few of the parish churches have anything which suggests a chancel. Usually the altar-table is placed against the eastern wall and set apart by rails on three sides. Pulpit, reading desk, and clerk's pew appear closer to the congregation, combined or on either side of the central aisle as in St. Mary-at-Hill, London, 1677 (Figure 19). The fonts

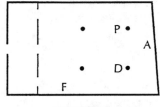

FIGURE 19

generally remained near the main entrance. The congregation, seated in high box pews on the floor of the nave or in the gallery, is as close as possible to the two main liturgical centers. The liturgical centers for the two sacraments and the offices and sermon remain distinct, yet none is hidden.

In a very real sense Wren's auditory church plan became the norm for most Anglican churches until the 1840s. Though it is

[17] Cf. R. H. Harrison, "Temporary Churches after the Great Fire," *Transactions of the Ecclesiological Society*, III (New Series) (1955–56), 251–8.

[18] For examples see Gerald Cobb, *The Old Churches of London* (3rd ed.; London: Batsford, 1948); Viktor Fürst, *The Architecture of Sir Christopher Wren* (London: Lund Humphries, 1956); E. F. Sekler, *Wren and His Place in European Architecture* (London: Faber & Faber, 1956).

difficult to generalize about buildings built over such an expanse of time, they basically were one-room auditory churches without chancels. The three-decker, the altar-table, and the font remained the important liturgical centers, each in its own distinct space as in the small church erected at Chislehampton in 1762 (Figure 20).

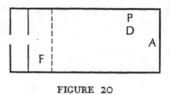

FIGURE 20

Many of these buildings were also central buildings, reflecting Wren's frequent use of a central plan with various elaborations.[19]

III

During the seventeenth and eighteenth centuries America served as a vast laboratory for experimentation on the architectural setting of Protestant worship. Every building provided an opportunity to start afresh, to investigate new possibilities. New challenges appeared in the use of materials neglected or scarce in Europe as well as the new functions a building might have in the total life of the community. In some areas churches were the only civic architecture.

It would be impossible to consider here all the experiments conducted in this country during the colonial period. Instead we shall discuss examples chosen from the two largest religious bodies in colonial America, the Church of England and the Puri-

[19] Cf. Marcus Whiffen, *Stuart and Georgian Churches: The Architecture of the Church of England Outside London 1603–1837* (London: Batsford, 1947).

tans. The Church of England, of course, is represented by the Protestant Episcopal tradition today; the Puritans, most directly by the Congregationalists, though much of what is said of them here applies to the Baptist and Presbyterian heritages. Some quite surprising differences can be seen by comparing the Anglican buildings and the Puritan ones even in the same colonies as each tradition developed its own architecture. The Anglicans, with a fixed liturgy, tried a great variety of experiments; the Puritans, with freedom in worship, show a remarkably fixed pattern in liturgical arrangement.

The Church of England in colonial America remained under the canon law of the Mother Country which provided that "all ministers . . . shall observe the Orders, Rites, and Ceremonies prescribed in the Book of Common Prayer . . . without either diminishing . . . or adding anything in the matter or form thereof." Although this left a fair degree of latitude in such matters as the frequency of holy communion (once the required three celebrations per year had been held), it did mean that basically the same services would be performed in every church. It is therefore all the more surprising to see the variety of experiments carried on to secure the most appropriate setting for worship according to the *Book of Common Prayer*. During the nineteenth century these colonial experiments were forgotten but they have a direct relevance in the contemporary search for forms in Protestant architecture.

From what little we know of the first few generations of Anglicans in America we can say that they were not particularly venturesome in their church architecture. Information gained from the ruins of the fifth church in Jamestown (1647), the second Bruton Parish Church, Williamsburg (1683), and the still existing St. Luke's, Smithfield, Va. (possibly built as early as 1632), indicates a strong conservatism. These early churches show an architecture of nostalgia, duplicating as much as possible the medieval parish church even to the extent of having wooden chancel screens across the east end of the buildings.[20]

Such conservatism was shed in the eighteenth century, particularly after Wren's contributions in England had become known. One can make some general statements about the furnishings of the buildings erected by Anglicans in eighteenth-century America.[21] In almost every instance the altar-table was shaped like a small table in form and reflected the changing styles in secular furnishings. It was usually covered with an altar cloth but was uncluttered by candles and crosses. If anything appeared on the altar-table it was more likely to be handsomely bound volumes of the Bible and the Prayer Book and the alms basin. In some cases there might be a painting to ornament the east end and the required Decalogue would often be accompanied by the Creed and Lord's Prayer. Other than these features the altar-tables were remarkably simple and unadorned. Almost invariably eighteenth-century Anglican churches had the altar-table enclosed by rails.

Although canon law required that the font be "of stone" and "set in the ancient usual places" the Bishop was far away and considerable freedom was exercised. Several wooden fonts have survived, and we know that in some churches silver baptismal basins were used, not unlike those of the Puritans. More often than not the font was likely to appear at the east end of the building where the sacrament could be performed in full view of the entire congregation. The font in this position is also found in a number of English churches of the same period, the advantage being that of stressing the congregational nature of the sacrament.

[20] Cf. James Grote Van Derpool "The Restoration of St. Luke's, Smithfield, Virginia," *Journal of the Society of Architectural Historians*, XVII (1958), 12–18; and H. C. Forman, *Jamestown and St. Mary's* (Baltimore: John Hopkins Press, 1938).

[21] Many of these furnishings and buildings are illustrated in Stephen P. Dorsey, *Early English Churches in America, 1607–1807* (New York: Oxford University Press, 1952).

In most churches of this period the dominant liturgical center was the pulpit and reading desk. Frequently this was a single center, the two-decker pulpit, or when combined with a clerk's pew, the three-decker as in King's Chapel, Boston (1717) or Trinity Church, Newport, R.I. (1725). Pulpit and desk might be separate from each other, but usually they remained in close proximity. In most cases they were by far the most prominent liturgical centers of the building and certainly the most used.

The main body of the church was filled with pews, especially the box pews popular in the eighteenth century. Frequently these were sold as private property and decorated according to the taste (or lack thereof) of the owner. Though the shapes could vary, they were often square or rectangular with a door opening onto the aisle. Frequently seats ran on three sides of the pew. This gave a certain mobility to the occupants since they could turn to face the opposite end of the building if necessary to look at a liturgical center different from the customary one. It gave the congregation more mobility in orientation than is possible in modern slip pews. It also insured that the family might sit together, enabling the parents to keep an eye on their offspring without other members of the congregation doing so.

Most of the churches erected in the eighteenth century have only a slight recess for a chancel or none at all. When a chancel does appear it was most likely to be a shallow rounded apse or one arm of a cruciform building. No chancel screens have survived, and in every case the space for worship is a single room. Frequently the communion rail defines the liturgical space about the altar and is often returned at the sides to allow pews to be placed to the left and right of the altar-table.

It is possible to detect at least six quite distinct types of experiments in liturgical arrangements in the eighteenth-century churches still surviving in America. One of the most interesting types is represented in St. Paul's Church, Wickford, R. I., built in 1707 (Figure 21). This building is a rectangle with the pulpit

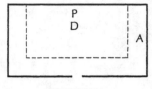

FIGURE 21

and reading desk in the center of one long wall opposite the main
entrance. Both are enclosed on three sides by pews. At one short
end of the building stands the altar-table beneath a gallery which
is carried around three sides of the church. The placement of the
pulpit suggests the Puritan arrangement of the time, but the pulpit and altar-table are at right angles to each other on the two
axes of the building. This arrangement probably indicates an in-
frequent use of the altar-table since it cannot be seen by half the
people in the gallery.

A second type appeared in St. James' Church, Goose Creek,
S. C., a rectangular building erected in 1711 (Figure 22). In this

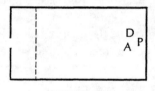

FIGURE 22

church a tall pulpit stands at the center of one short end of the
building. Directly below and in front of it stands the altar-table,
enclosed by the semicircular rails. Beside the pulpit and altar-
table and also within the rails stands the reading desk. The chief
advantage of such an arrangement was that it brought all the liturgical centers together in a place easily seen by the entire congregation. The pulpit, as the dominant center, is in front of a round-
headed pulpit window and on either side appear the Decalogue,

the Lord's Prayer, and the Creed. A sub-type appears in Christ Church, Duanesberg, N. Y. (1789), where the altar-table is beside the central two-decker pulpit, both against the east wall. Pulpit-centered arrangements have now almost disappeared from the Episcopal Church.

Only one example has survived in America of a type fairly common in the eighteenth century. In Trinity Church, Newport, R. I. (built in 1725) a tall wineglass pulpit, reading desk, and clerk's pew stand in the central aisle of the church directly in front of the altar-table (Figure 23). The building is a rectangle,

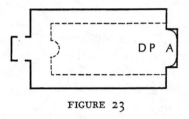

FIGURE 23

these liturgical centers appearing at one of the short ends with a gallery around the other three sides. A silver baptismal basin was used in this building instead of a font. Although it might seem that the pulpit would obscure the view of the altar-table, this does not happen. The congregation sits in box pews on either side of the central aisle or in the galleries and easily sees past the pulpit to the altar-table. Such an arrangement was once found in Old North Church, Boston (1723) and in some of the early Methodist chapels in England.

A fourth type appeared in the cruciform type, nowhere more magnificently illustrated than in Christ Church, Lancaster County, Va., erected in 1732 (Figure 24). There are box pews throughout this building, neatly divided by two aisles on the axes. The altar-table appears in the eastern arm. By its side is a marble font. The three-decker pulpit is at the southwestern cor-

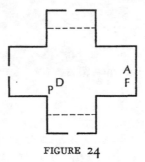

FIGURE 24

ner of the crossing, facing the crossing. Other examples of the same type of building place the pulpit at the southeast angle of the crossing (Abingdon Church, Gloucester County; Aquia Church, Stafford County; and Bruton, Williamsburg, all in Virginia). There are parallels with the cruciform churches in the Reformed churches of Europe except that in these Anglican churches a railed-in altar-table occupies the eastern arm. A considerable number of people can be brought close to the liturgical centers by this arrangement, particularly when three of the arms contain galleries.

Another type appears in Donation Church, Princess Anne County, Va., erected in 1736 (Figure 25). In this rectangular

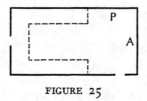

FIGURE 25

building, the altar-table is in the center of the east end. Directly in front of the rails is an aisle across the church and the pulpit appears in the north end of this against the wall. Although there is no structural chancel, the pulpit is placed as if it were just beyond where the chancel screen would have been in a medieval church. A similar location evidently occurred in St. Luke's, Smithfield, Va., where a chancel screen is known to have existed.

One of the most interesting types appears in only two surviving churches, St. Peter's, Philadelphia, 1758 (Figure 26) and

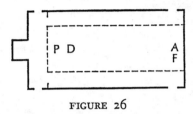

FIGURE 26

Pompion Hill Chapel above the Cooper River in South Carolina (1763). In both of these buildings, the one a sophisticated city church, the other a remote country chapel of ease, altar-table and pulpit are at opposite ends of rectangular structures. At St. Peter's, box pews made it possible for the congregation to face whichever liturgical center was being used, the pulpit and reading desk in the west or the altar-table and font in the east. At Pompion Hill the slip pews run parallel to the long sides of the building. Some indication of the relative importance of pulpit and altar-table here is seen in the fact that the pews near the pulpit were painted white whereas those near the altar-table were painted brown and used by slaves.

Most likely other arrangements were tried but have disappeared. It is remarkable that so many varieties did appear in the eighteenth century, particularly in the light of the uniformity which became a characteristic of Anglican churches throughout the world after the Cambridge Movement of the nineteenth century. In general, one sees in the eighteenth-century experiments an attempt to bring the liturgical centers, particularly the pulpit and desk, close to the people so that all may see, hear, and take part in worship.

Among the Puritans quite a different situation prevailed. They succeeded quite early in establishing a suitable liturgical arrangement and it was retained with remarkable unanimity though the buildings considerably changed. The Puritan liturgical centers included a tall pulpit with the congregation gathered about it on the main floor and in an encircling gallery. Directly in front of the pulpit was usually a pew occupied by the elders or deacons. Before this stood the altar-table upon which a baptismal basin could be placed. And that was all. It was the simplest and most direct arrangement possible for Puritan worship.

Some generalizations can be made about these buildings. The entire service was led from the pulpit except during the sacraments. Preaching, "being the power of God unto salvation," naturally was a most important part of the service. This importance was reflected in the size of the pulpits, some of them being as much as twelve feet high. There might be a cushion on the pulpit for the Bible and an hourglass to time the sermon. Since everything else in the building was subordinate to the pulpit, it formed the dominant architectural focus. Frequently, there was a sounding board above the pulpit suspended from the ceiling or projecting from the wall. Round-headed windows behind the pulpit added to its elegance. Some of the most beautiful pulpits were of the wineglass variety though later versions were perched upon four or more legs. Occasionally two curving staircases swept up from either side. Many of these eighteenth-century pulpits are esthetic triumphs, far more pleasing than the platform and desk pulpit which replaced them in the next century.

The Lord's supper was frequently celebrated monthly among Congregationalists and quarterly among Presbyterians. In New England it seems likely that it was received in the pews, the bread and wine being passed to the people in the pews by the deacons. In the words of John Cotton, "Ceremonies wee use none" and this simplicity was reflected in the small plain tables, sometimes just a leaf was hinged on the elder's pew. Thus the elder could sit behind the table and face the congregation across it at sacrament time. Beautiful examples of communion silver have survived. They include chalices, flagons, and cups, as well as baptismal basins.[22]

One of the most common characteristics of Puritan meetinghouses was the presence of galleries. Their purpose, of course, was to bring the congregation as close as possible to the pulpit. The presence of galleries accounts, in part, for the excessive height of the pulpit. A common form of the gallery was the so-called horseshoe gallery, reaching around the sides that did not contain the pulpit. In a few cases there were two tiers of galleries. Though the galleries might have either slip pews or box pews, the floor of the church was almost certain to have box pews.

These colonial meetinghouses were elegant in their simplicity. There were no traditional ecclesiastical symbols but there was a directness in building for a specific type of worship. Clean, well-lighted, they concentrated on the essentials of Puritan worship, the hearing of God's Word, with no distractions. For their purposes they were wonderfully successful examples of liturgical architecture.

During the seventeenth and eighteenth centuries there was a series of four stages in the evolution of the New England meetinghouse now so familiar on calendars and Christmas cards. The earliest buildings were evidently quite primitive. Very little is known about these buildings save that they were often fortified against Indian attack. During the seventeenth century they were replaced by larger wooden buildings sometimes square, or nearly so, in plan (Figure 27). Opposite the main entrance stood the pulpit set in the center of the wall. Galleries seem to have been customary. Only one example of this type of building has survived, Old Ship Church in Hingham, Mass., built in 1681. Enough

[22] Cf. *American Church Silver of the Seventeenth and Eighteenth Centuries with a Few Pieces of Domestic Plate* (Boston: Museum of Fine Arts, 1911).

FIGURE 27

documentary evidence is available, however, to show that it was not an isolated example. Plain and nearly square, Old Ship Church has a tall pulpit with a pulpit window behind and an old hourglass has been preserved. A pew for elders and deacons appears below the pulpit as does the small altar-table.

In the years after 1700 these buildings were replaced by others which nevertheless retained the same arrangement of liturgical centers (Figure 28). In this third type the building is rectangular

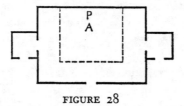

FIGURE 28

with the pulpit set in the middle of one long side. There is a touch of the medieval nave with the pulpit in the middle of one side. Architecturally the buildings built during the eighteenth century show increasing sophistication. The towers, which rise from the ground, betray the influence of Wren, though in America wood and brick were substituted for the stone used in England. Old South Church in Boston (1729) shows the Puritans seeking to match the elegance of the Anglican Old North Church (1723). Both have towers at one end, round-headed windows, and magnificent interior woodwork, but Old South is true to its tradition in orienting the interior about a pulpit in the center of a long side. Many buildings of this type have a very domestic appearance on the exterior. Galleries made it difficult to provide full-length windows so most of the exteriors have two rows of windows similar to homes of the period. A few examples of this type of building remain scattered in the New England states, particularly Farmington, Conn. (1771); Amesbury, Mass. (1785); Alna, Me. (1789); Newport, R. I. (1729); Sandown, N. H. (1774); and Rockingham, Vt. (1787).[23]

The final and most familiar type emerged in the buildings built after the Revolutionary War. In these the orientation has been changed so that the pulpit appears in the center of a short side of the rectangle opposite the main entrance (Figure 29). Frequently

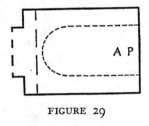

FIGURE 29

the rooms are only a bit longer than wide so that the basic interior is not far removed from a square. However, a narthex or portico has been added to the end opposite the pulpit producing a rectangular building. The portico and tower over it were due to the influence of James Gibbs, an architect who worked in England developing this composition so familiar on many meetinghouses. Galleries were usually present, often in horseshoe form.

It should be noticed that none of these buildings had chancels

[23] Illustrations and descriptions of the Connecticut examples appear in J. Frederick Kelly, *Early Connecticut Meetinghouses: Being an Account of the Church Edifices Built before 1830 Based Chiefly upon Town and Parish Records* (New York: Columbia University Press, 1948), 2 vols.

or even a suggestion of a chancel, quite unlike the modern "re-productions" of them. A single liturgical arrangement, that of central pulpit and altar-table below it, persisted for over a hundred and fifty years before being superseded. Choirs and organs were unknown during much of this period in Congregational churches. The introduction of choirs and a new concept of preaching replaced the traditional Puritan arrangement in the mid-nineteenth century.

A special type of church, the college chapel, shows a distinctive form in both Anglican and Puritan colleges. The chapel built at the College of William and Mary in 1732 may have had the traditional collegiate arrangement: stalls parallel to the long sides and the altar-table at one end opposite the entrance. At Harvard, Holden Chapel (built 1742–44) had this seating arrangement but with a reading desk at the end opposite the door.

IV

Two other Protestant traditions produced distinctive buildings: the Quakers and the Methodists. The Quakers developed the most radical liturgical arrangement of all Protestant groups and held to it with remarkable consistency. Quaker worship actually is one of the most highly corporate forms of worship. According to Robert Barclay, in the silent waiting upon God of Quaker worship,

God reveals himself and draweth near to every individual, and so he is in the midst in the general, whereby each not only partakes of the particular refreshment and strength which comes from the good in himself, but is a sharer in the whole body, as being a living member of the body, having a joint fellowship and communion with all.[24]

Barclay proceeds to liken Quaker worship to the way "many candles lighted, and put in one place, do greatly augment the

[24] *An Apology for the True Christian Divinity.* (Manchester: William Irwin, 1869), p. 224.

light." These principles are reflected remarkably well in the Quaker meetinghouses of the colonial period.

No liturgical centers appear but instead the entire building has become liturgical space. All persons present participate fully and equally in the worship of the meeting. Thus the only furnishings are the benches for the worshipers. Frequently the main body of benches faces a bench or two for the elders of the meeting and other rows of benches on the floor level or in galleries may flank the main body of benches.

Perhaps as early as the seventeenth century the Quaker meetinghouse type became fixed. It was usually a rectangle with two main entrances. Since the women sometimes met separately (having different concerns), there was often a movable partition down the middle (width) of the building as in the Medford, N. J. meetinghouse erected in 1814 (Figure 30). Men and women

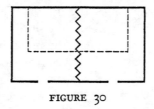

FIGURE 30

might use separate entrances. The division of the sexes was attempted in many Protestant denominations. The first *Book of Common Prayer* (1549) provided for separation of the men and women at communion; in the eighteenth century Wesley made an effort to divide them at worship and some Anglicans tried to do likewise in the nineteenth century. But only the Quakers succeeded in accomplishing this supernatural task and they gave it up in the nineteenth century.

The buildings themselves were models of simplicity and their stonework or brick has a very great appeal to modern eyes. In turning the entire space into liturgical space the Quakers accomplished the abolition of any exclusive liturgical space for clergy and truly made it apparent that all the people of God performed a ministry in common worship.

Methodism dates from the eighteenth century, having originated as a movement within the Church of England under the leadership of John and Charles Wesley. This relationship to the Church of England is important to remember for the early Methodist people conceived of their worship largely as an adjunct to that of the Established Church. Their services were intended to supplement, not to supplant, the Anglican services. Indeed Methodist services during "church-hours" were frowned upon. The *Large Minutes* of the 1770 Conference preferred to refer to the Methodist buildings as "preaching-houses." [25] This indicates their essential function, to serve as the locale for preaching services but not to replace the parish church for the sacraments. In the *Minutes* of 1766 Wesley declared that Methodist worship was "not such as supersedes the Church [Anglican] Service. We never designed it should." [26] The Methodist preaching-houses originally served a function not too unlike the preaching churches erected by the friars in the thirteenth and fourteenth centuries.

In a few of the Methodist chapels it became customary to administer communion. Wesley had become convinced by 1764 that no consecration was necessary or lawful other than holding public worship in a building.[27] Accordingly altar-tables and rails began to appear in the Methodist buildings though they may have had little use during Wesley's lifetime except when an ordained minister was present. The Methodist services centered in preach-

---

[25] *Minutes of the Methodist Conferences, from the First, Held in London, by The Late Rev. John Wesley, A.M. in the Year 1744* (London: John Mason, 1862), I, 540.

[26] Ibid. I, 59.

[27] *Journal of the Rev. John Wesley, A.M.* edited by Nehemiah Curnock (Standard ed.; New York: Eaton and Mains, n.d.), Vol. V, August 20, 1764 and February 28, 1772.

ing, a factor reflected in the invariably prominent pulpit. Hymn singing was an important part of Methodist worship. Anthems were forbidden, however, "because they cannot be properly called joint-worship" (*Minutes*, 1787).[28]

The early Methodist preaching-houses and chapels are a good index to Wesley's ideas of worship since his supervision extended to the architecture of these buildings as well as to their uses. Before any building had been erected for Methodist worship, and long afterwards, field preaching was popular, although the *Minutes* of 1744 caution: "Yet (to avoid giving any needless offence) we never preach *without* doors, when we can with conveniency preach *within*." [29] In many areas the poverty of the Methodist people made it impossible to erect preaching-houses. Private homes, barns, inns, old theaters, and other buildings were used as Methodist preaching-houses. When funds did permit, several distinctive types of buildings were erected.

The most remarkable of these was the octagon. The inspiration for building in this shape seems to have come from Wesley's visit to Norwich in 1757 when he saw the octagonal meetinghouse completed by nonconformists there the year before (Figure 31).

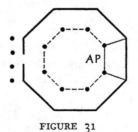

FIGURE 31

With Wesley's powerful authority behind it, this type of building was widely adopted by Methodists. At least a dozen such

[28] *Minutes*, I, 203.
[29] Ibid. I, 23.

buildings were erected between 1760 and 1770. The Conference *Minutes* of 1770 and following years carried instructions to "build all preaching-houses, if the ground will admit, in the octagon form. It is the best for the voice, and on many accounts more commodious than any other." [30] These two features—the assumed superiority for preaching purposes, and the increased accommodation made possible by galleries on seven sides—were probably Wesley's chief reasons for building octagons. This shape does not seem to have been used much among American Methodists.

Though the octagon had an early popularity in English Methodism, it was eventually replaced by rectangular buildings. Actually the earliest Methodist preaching-house, the New Room in Bristol, 1739 (Figure 32) is of a roughly rectangular shape as are

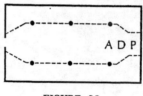

FIGURE 32

the American buildings. The Bristol building, still very much in its original condition, has a two-decker pulpit in the center of one short end. In front of the pulpit and reading desk is a platform enclosed by a rail containing the altar-table. There are galleries on the two long sides.

The most famous early Methodist chapel, the City Road Chapel in London, was opened in 1778 (Figure 33). It is significant that it was designated a chapel instead of a preaching-house. In liturgical arrangement it was similar to many eighteenth-century Anglican churches. Evidently it fulfilled for Methodists

[30] Ibid. I, 612.

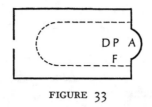

FIGURE 33

many of the functions of a parish church, and an episcopally ordained minister was usually present to administer the sacraments.
The presence here of a stone baptismal font at an early date indicates an exceptional development of Methodist independence. In
its original form, City Road Chapel was a plain building with
galleries on three sides and a shallow apse on the fourth. The apse
contains an altar-table and rails. Directly in front of it stands the
pulpit, once a three-decker now shorn of the top five feet of its
former fifteen-foot height. A few examples of this arrangement
survive in Methodist chapels but in most instances the altar-table
evidently stood in front of the pulpit. City Road Chapel had a
great influence on subsequent Methodist chapels, especially after
the ruling of the 1790 Conference, "Every house larger than the
Bath house is to be built on the plan of the new chapel in London,
both within and without." [31]

After Wesley's death, Methodism lost much of its distinctive
emphasis on frequent communion. Methodists ceased going to the
parish church for the sacrament and it was neglected in the Methodist chapels. There is little to distinguish the Methodist chapels
of the nineteenth century from those of other nonconformists
except the altar rail. The Anglican practice of kneeling at the rail
survived in Methodism.

Since most of the early Methodists were poor, the chapels were
often very simple. The *Minutes* of the 1780 Conference ordered,
"Let all preaching-houses be built plain and decent; but not more

[31] Ibid. I, 242.

expensive than is absolutely unavoidable; otherwise the necessity of raising money will make rich men necessary to us. But if so, we must be dependent upon them, yea, and governed by them. And then farewell to Methodist discipline, if not doctrine too." [32] Such dangers were guarded against in the eighteenth century. Symbolism and decorations were absent. When the image of an angel with a trumpet had somehow been erected over the pulpit in the Halifax preaching-house it was an offense to the weaker brethren and had to be removed and burnt.[33] This is a bit strange as such a figure was an appropriate symbol of the preached word and was popular among French Protestants. English Puritanism, however, had dispensed with even this much symbolism. Thus early Methodism combined Puritanical severity with the altar rails of Laud's high churchmanship, a symbol of the combination of these two traditions in Methodism.

V

In this brief survey some common traits can be seen in the Protestant experiments of the sixteenth, seventeenth, and eighteenth centuries. Foremost of these was a willingness to experiment at least until a completely adequate form was secured. The more complex and varied the liturgical life of a tradition was, the more difficult it was to find the optimum form. Thus the American Puritans early achieved a satisfactory arrangement, while Lutherans and Anglicans continued to explore new possibilities throughout this period. In a way this is indicative of Protestant theology, which is unwilling to concede an absolute character to a theological formulation. The fear that according finality to any theological statement would be basically idolatrous is repeated in the continual search for more adequate liturgical arrangements.

[32] Ibid. I, 613.

[33] *Journal*, April 15, 1779.

One of the dominant characteristics of the buildings cited above is the preponderance of a central type building. Chancels had become largely superfluous in most Protestant traditions by the eighteenth century. The churches erected were one-room churches with a strong focus on the central space. The result was that of combining the liturgical space occupied by the congregation as closely as possible with that used by the clergy. Emphasis was placed on the whole people of God, hearing, seeing, and doing the liturgy. It should be pointed out that most of the Roman Catholic churches built in southern Europe during this time, were also central churches. The mass was made magnificent and visible, and some orders built churches designed for frequent preaching. If the Middle Ages suggested the mystery of the mass, the baroque era was more inclined to suggest the dramatic qualities of Roman Catholic worship. Although both Protestants and Catholics did build some longitudinal buildings during these centuries, the central church type came into its own during this period.

V

Behind the Current Stalemate

In the last one hundred years two types of liturgical arrangements have come to dominate Protestant church building to the point of becoming standard patterns. So prevalent have these two types become that, until recently, further experiments were few and far between and even now their number is only slowly increasing. One of the two dominant types is the concert stage arrangement with tiers of choir stalls behind a pulpit platform at the foot of which appears the altar-table. The other type is the so-called divided chancel with the choir stalls and altar-table within the chancel and the pulpit at one side of its entrance. In both cases the liturgical space allotted to the congregation tends to be similar, a long rectangular nave.

It is interesting that these two types have come to have such a widespread usage in contemporary Protestantism that it is often impossible to tell the denomination for which a building is intended simply by looking at the interior. In itself this is an indication of indifference to strong denominational traditions in worship. By and large the nineteenth and twentieth centuries saw the gradual assimilation of each other's traditions in worship by the various denominations. Though they once would have been obviously distinct, there is often little today to distinguish buildings erected for worship by Presbyterians, Lutherans, and Episcopalians.

The differences which appear in the choice of the concert stage or divided chancel arrangements more often seem to be by-products of social and cultural matters than theological ones. Ultimately, the difference is between the relative impact of two nineteenth-century movements on the culture of a region. Thus the relative importance of revivalism or romanticism as cultural patterns is often more important than the denominational traditions which have eroded away and been forgotten.

In this respect the nineteenth and twentieth centuries represent a distinct break from the patterns prevalent in the three previous centuries. Previously experimentation had been common except where a well-recognized denominational pattern had been established. Indeed experimentation had become almost a tradition in itself for Anglicans and Lutherans. Yet even these experiments grew out of the denominations' particular traditions so that the relative importance of the liturgical centers helped give a distinct quality to the buildings of each group. The loss of this distinctiveness and the paucity of experiments mark the nineteenth and twentieth centuries off from those preceding.

In a sense, what happened in church architecture is symptomatic of some of the profound changes occurring in Protestant worship in the nineteenth and early twentieth centuries. This period saw a tendency toward the breakdown of the emphasis on corporate action in common worship which the reformers sought to achieve. The nineteenth century succeeded in overturning many of the principles of the Reformation relating to worship while fervently professing faithfulness to the reformers. One of the cardinal notes of the modern Liturgical Movement has been a reversal of the strong individualism which came to characterize the approach to worship during the last century. In so doing the

Movement joins hands with the reformers and the early Church but remains highly critical of the individualism of the nineteenth century and late Middle Ages.

Strangely enough, some of the sources of this individualism seem at first glance to have little in common. Revivalism was a popular movement which rarely concerned itself with much intellectual sophistication. On the other hand, romanticism was highly sophisticated and reflected in many of the great minds of the century. Yet in worship both led to a strong stress on the importance of feeling and a tendency to exalt the individual.

At the same time the congregation assumed an increasingly passive role as more and more of the service was performed by the clergy or choir. Although esthetically Protestant worship has improved considerably in the last century and a half, it has often been at the loss of congregational participation. An increasing professionalism has shown itself as congregations allow minister and choir to perform most of the acts of worship except for a few half-hearted hymns.

Architecturally this is expressed in the two dominant building types. Both are usually longitudinal buildings with the implicit hierarchical distinctions between clergy and people which this type often involves. In both cases the main liturgical centers are separated from the congregation by both vertical and horizontal distinctions. Both concert stage and divided chancel arrangements remove the leaders of worship into liturgical space to which the rest of the congregation has no direct access except when receiving communion. Thus the congregation is encouraged to assume a spectator role while watching and listening to minister and choir during the service.

It is a bit surprising that such arrangements could have so firm a grip on the imagination of the average Protestant. Unconsciously we have allowed nineteenth-century concepts of worship to lull us, so we are not fully aware of what has been lost. Yet this stalemate continues with the constant repetition of buildings quite inadequate for Protestant worship. The concert stage and the divided chancel arrangements certainly do not express the concepts of worship held by the sixteenth-century reformers and are equally foreign to the best liturgical thought of our own time. And yet these stereotyped arrangements are repeated in hundreds of new churches each year.

I

Modern American Protestantism is affected in almost every area of Church life by the revivalism of the nineteenth century. Indeed it was mass evangelism of the revivalistic type which changed America from a nation with a Christian minority to a nation in which most of the population belongs to a Church.[1] Though the revival pattern has died out in many denominations, the strengths and weaknesses of this form of evangelism have become a permanent part of American Christianity. This is especially true in relation to worship where many of the basic presuppositions of revivalism linger on even where revivals are most vehemently repudiated.

Many of the major patterns of nineteenth-century revivalism originated on the frontier. One of the most successful institutions of frontier revivalism was the camp meeting in which thousands of people gathered from isolated farms, camping on the grounds for several days at a time. For the rough and exuberant pioneers, camp meeting time was a time of great emotional intensity, occasionally accompanied by awesome physical manifestations of the feelings experienced. The emotional sobriety of the great eighteenth-century evangelist, Jonathan Edwards, was often forgotten and preachers addressed their hearers on a highly emotional level as the most direct means of producing conversions.

At times the camp meeting situation saw a blurring of denomi-

[1] For an interesting discussion see Franklin H. Littell, *From State Church to Pluralism* (New York: Doubleday, 1962), Ch. II.

national traditions as evangelists of various Churches cooperated on the same campgrounds. People moved freely from preacher to preacher. The preaching was similar: a call to repentance and an exhortation to accept Christ. It is interesting that a celebration of the Lord's supper often climaxed the meetings, the different groups tending to separate for these occasions. Evidently only a minority of those present communicated, but the sacrament often was the occasion of further conversions. In the words of one contemporary: "The work is greatest on sacramental occasions." [2] Increasingly, denominational traditions fell victim to the practical expediency of the frontier. At times this caused schisms within denominations. Several groups broke off from the Presbyterians and eventually formed another denomination, the Disciples of Christ. The Lord's supper became a part of the normal Sunday service of this group. The general practice among the Disciples of Christ has been to receive communion in the pews and the altar-table is almost always a free-standing table. A sunken baptistery is usually provided for immersion.

The keynote of revivalism was that of producing a conversion, in which a person's total being was profoundly changed. Francis Asbury recorded a typical occasion in his *Journal:* "I judge two hundred souls were made the subjects of grace in its various operations of conviction, conversion, sanctification, and reclamation." [3] It is not strange that the primary emphasis in revivalism was upon the individual and his conversion experience. One attended revivals until converted, then he labored to convert others. Beside such an earnest concern for producing converts, worship as an offering to God seemed to be only a side issue. Even the Church itself became somewhat of an option except for

[2] Colonel Robert Patterson, quoted by H. Shelton Smith, Robert T. Handy, and Lefferts A. Loetscher in *American Christianity: an Historical Interpretation with Representative Documents* (New York: Scribners, 1960), I, 569.

[3] *The Journal and Letters of Francis Asbury,* edited by Elmer T. Clark (Nashville: Abingdon, 1958), II, 505-6.

providing the means to continue the work of extending revivals. It is not strange that in such a situation worship became a means to an end—producing conversions—rather than an end in itself. Worship was utilized primarily for inducing conversion experiences rather than the offering of a sacrifice of praise and thanksgiving by God's people.

Revivalism did not long remain confined to the frontier though many of its characteristics were developed in such an environment. It was the introduction of the revival system among the churches of the East Coast that brought revivalism into the main stream of American Protestant life. By this time it had developed into a coherent pattern. Probably no one deserves more credit for bringing the frontier practices of revivalism into the church life of the East than Charles G. Finney. Converted in upstate New York, where he then worked as a revivalist of great power, Finney eventually came to New York City and popularized many of the practices of revivalism despite opposition from his fellow Presbyterians. Finney referred to his methods as the "new measures" though most had not been his invention. In his *Lectures on Revivals of Religion* (1835) he made very clear his willingness to dispense with traditional forms of worship if they did not produce conversions:

The fact is, that God has established, in no church, any particular *form*, or manner of worship, for promoting the interests of religion. The scriptures are entirely silent on these subjects, under the gospel dispensation, and the church is left to exercise her own discretion in relation to all such matters.[4]

Though one may question whether worship exists "for promoting the interests of religion," there can be no mistaking the clear practical intention Finney had of using those measures which produce conversions and of discarding those which he considered ineffectual.

[4] *Lectures on Revivals of Religion*, edited by William G. McLoughlin (Cambridge, Mass.: Harvard University Press, 1960), p. 276.

The consequences are quite clear. One stresses all means available for bringing the individual to conversion. Particularly useful are those which condition him emotionally to accept the offer of salvation. Choral singing became an important part of revivalism and song leaders and choirs remain a vital part of contemporary revivals. The approach to the worshiper is emotional, subjective, and individualistic. And very few contemporary Protestant congregations are free of the same approach to the public worship of the church today.

The consequences for church architecture were much more far-reaching than are usually realized. Not only did revivalism lead to a new liturgical arrangement but eventually to a quite new concept of the basic purposes of a church building.

Revivalism tended to focus on the development of pulpit personalities, with a lessening of the objective sense of the sermon as an exposition of the Scriptures through which God addressed men. It is interesting to trace the shrinking of the pulpit and the expanding of the pulpit platform upon which it stood as revivalistic preaching spread. Until the beginning of the nineteenth century Protestant pulpits were usually of the "tub" type, a rather large structure in which the preacher stood. Often a high sounding board made the preacher seem rather diminutive. Yet in a sense these huge pulpits gave a note of authority to the preached word which transcended the individual preacher. (This can be easily gauged by preaching without a pulpit before a congregation accustomed to one, and seeing how the sermon becomes a personal talk.) Many great revivalist preachers preferred a small desk-like pulpit big enough to hold only their notes. But they relished a large platform on which to make sorties in all directions as they pleaded for conversions.

Certainly the pulpit platform gave room for histrionics and also made it possible for the preacher to kneel at any point on the stage, especially if he found it necessary to pray for the conversion of a particular individual. It also became quite common for several people to lead a service of worship. There might be a song leader and a visiting minister besides the pastor. Accommodation for these were provided by three large chairs which had a much more practical use than representing the Trinity. Some of these chairs from pulpit platforms will be museum pieces in the twenty-first century if not destroyed before then.

A very conspicuous addition was in the provision of space for choirs and organs. Puritanism had resisted these innovations throughout the seventeenth and much of the eighteenth centuries. But revivalism was never prone to turn down any effective measure and it was realized that choirs and organ music could be most useful in inducing the feelings associated with worship. The arrangement adopted for the choir was usually a semicircle of tiers of seats facing the congregation. Musically it was probably as good as any and is familiar today on the concert stage. The organ console usually was at the base of the choir seats and the organ pipes towered over all with their gilt glory.

A further consequence was a growing awareness of the power of a building in creating a worshipful atmosphere. This was to have its fullest expression in the twentieth century when the emotive factors of architecture were used skillfully to induce a mood in which conversion would be encouraged. Pictorial stained glass windows blossomed in every building; painted organ pipes and brass fixtures added to the religious atmosphere. In a way it was an interesting reversal of the Puritan fear of art and music as dangerous distractions from hearing the Word of God. Forgotten was the old Puritan reticence which had avoided decorative art and so sternly denounced "the squeaking of chanting choristers . . . imitating the fashion and manner of Antichrist the Pope." The congregation was increasingly a passive audience for whom worship was something done for them and to them by experts. The mood-setting beauties of the building and the music conditioned the congregation for worship but they did less and less as active participants. It is no accident that the part of the building occupied by the congregation was designed as an audience chamber much like that of a theater, and the pulpit platform and choir stalls resembled a stage.

In a number of old meetinghouses the old pulpit gave way to a pulpit platform complete with desk pulpit, and the sacrosanct three chairs. Often the building had to be enlarged to accommodate a choir and the addition of ornate organ pipes was the last blow to the fine austerity of many of these buildings. The Victorians, like nature, could not stand a vacuum.

It was not long, of course, before churches were built specifically under the influence of the revival system. They are often referred to, even today, as the "auditorium" and the term is expressive. As the term suggests, they are largely used as a place where the congregation hears worship. The concept is far from that of Wren's auditory church where the congregation was meant to be actively engaged in the acts of the liturgy as well as hearing the sermon.

Finney himself took a hand in designing Broadway Tabernacle in New York City. It was a large building with a gallery encircling the interior and a platform projecting onto the floor of the lower level. Tall organ pipes provided the backdrop for the platform. The size of many such buildings made any real sense of intimacy impossible. Hundreds of people had to be accommodated so they could see and hear the preacher. Generally galleries were necessary to seat worshipers in the larger churches. Pulpit platform and concert choir became standard arrangements (Figure 34). In the case of Baptist churches provision had to be made for a large baptistery often at the rear of the platform. This usually took the form of a sunken tank with steps leading down into it. Below the pulpit stood the altar-table, an inconspicuous furnishing.

One of the most prevalent sub-types developing out of the concert stage arrangement was the so-called Akron plan. Originated soon after the Civil War, it seems to have been the inven-

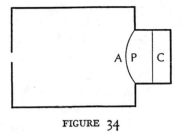

FIGURE 34

tion of a Mr. Lewis Miller and was first used in the First Methodist Episcopal Church of Akron, O. It was the product of an effort to provide a setting for Sunday Schools in which "opening exercises" could be conducted and then separate classes held. The Akron plan consisted of a hall with a horseshoe gallery. Both ground floor and gallery could be divided into classrooms by sliding partitions or opened for worship. Through the "opening exercises" the Sunday School came to have its own worship, often becoming a church within the church. Usually the Sunday School unit opened directly into the auditorium by means of sliding doors and often the gallery might be carried through into the auditorium. In its most common form the Akron plan included a pulpit platform wedged into one corner of the building (Figure 35). On this stood the pulpit, the inevitable pulpit chairs, and behind rose the concert choir and the organ pipes. On the lowest level stood a small altar-table, upon which a baptismal basin might be found on many Sundays. Usually the floor sloped downwards toward the pulpit platform. On overflow occasions

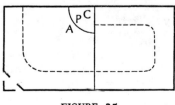

FIGURE 35

the partitions were opened and worshipers could sit in the Sunday School rooms.

An enthusiastic writer wrote half a century ago: "Church architecture in America—more especially that of the non-ritual church—has been completely revolutionized by this influence." [5] Certainly the Akron plan had a tremendous influence for half a century or more. Books were published illustrating its arrangement and singing its praises.[6] Many of these buildings are still in existence but since World War II hundreds have been remodeled so their original arrangement is unrecognizable. Indeed a number of articles and chapters in books on church building have raised the question, "What to do with the Akron plan?" Actually, for the type of worship for which it was created, the Akron plan was admirably suited, much more so than the building type which has so frequently superseded it. As one of its champions pointed out, "The strong point of this building—and this is the essential test of any building—is its utility in the highest sense. . . . Such completeness and comprehensiveness is almost without parallel among the inventions of man." [7] Divorced of its eclectic styles, the Akron plan is quite adequate for those groups whose concept of worship is hearing the minister and the choir, though many contemporary Protestants may care to question such a concept of worship.

In the last fifty years the Akron plan has been almost completely superseded by churches which place the Sunday School in separate rooms or even separate buildings, and quite different

[5] Marion Lawrence, "The Akron Plan—Its Genesis, History and Development," *Thirty-Second Annual Report of the Board of Church Extension of the Methodist Episcopal Church, South* (n.p., 1914), p. 270.

[6] Cf. W. H. Brearley, *Architect's Plans, Specifications, and Builders Estimate for an Improved Bible-School Building and Church Edifice Combined* ([Detroit?], 1881); and Sidney J. Osgood, *Churches* (Grand Rapids: Dean Printing and Publishing Co., 1893).

[7] Lawrence, "The Akron Plan . . ." p. 271.

concepts influence the design of classrooms. The auditorium is now usually a rectangle. At one short side is the pulpit platform and choir seats. The chief change seems to be that the choir robes are a bit gaudier and the organ pipes more subdued. Yet the question remains whether there is any real advantage in the congregation's being able to see either choir or pipes. Usually a small communion table appears on the floor of the church below the pulpit. Increasingly it is laden down with brass candlesticks and a cross or flowers. In Methodist churches an altar rail encircles the platform. So persistent has this become that Methodists who build divided chancels still place the rail outside the chancel even though the altar-table has retreated in the opposite direction. For Baptists and other groups a large baptistery may be located behind the pulpit or behind the choir. It seems to be virtually impossible to secure a location for the baptistery which will not be awkward on the numerous Sundays when it is not used. It is usually treated as an occasional liturgical center and concealed by drapes or by other means when not in use. It calls baptism to mind only when actually being used. The problem is compounded since all that the congregation can see during baptism is the empty space above the tank. Further experiments as to the design and location of the type of baptistery used for immersion are necessary.

Many of the concert stage type buildings being built today are well decorated and provided with emotive factors, particularly those involving the control of lights. This, of course, is in full keeping with the tendency of the revival tradition to emphasize the subjective approach to worship as basically a matter of feeling.

The liturgical space allotted to the congregation is most often the conventional theater arrangement. The pulpit platform tends to be a stage and the congregation occupies the place of an audience. The congregation rarely has any direct access to the liturgical centers themselves. No better example could be given of the passivity of the congregation than that they are willing to assume the role of spectators rather than be actors on stage. In itself this is an architectural denial of the ministry of all the faithful and a symptom of what has happened in much of Protestant worship.

II

It would seem at first glance that romanticism had little in common with revivalism. Yet both were imbued with the same spirit of individual expression. "The folk religion of the exuberant, optimistic, and undisciplined frontier represented a bizarre, but nonetheless genuine, expression to the spirit of romanticism." [8] Yet the romanticism which finally found its expression in American church building came from the opposite end of the ecclesiastical spectrum from that of revivalism. The total effect of both, though, has been a stress on worship as a subjective matter of feeling affecting men as individuals.

Romanticism in church architecture is usually associated with the revival of gothic architecture. It is interesting to trace the course of this period in the history of taste because it gives a good index of the concepts of worship. One of the first gothic churches in America was built by John Henry Hopkins as rector of Trinity Episcopal Church in Pittsburgh, Pa.[9] The new building, erected in 1823, replaced an earlier octagonal church. The arrangement of Hopkins's new church reflects the experiments of the eighteenth century. The building was basically a rectangle with galleries on three sides. In a slight recess at one end stood a

[8] Ralph H. Gabriel, "Evangelical Religion and Popular Romanticism in Early Nineteenth Century America," *Church History*, XIX (1950), 39.

[9] For more detail on Hopkins, cf. James F. White, "Theology and Architecture in America: A Study of Three Leaders," in *A Miscellany of American Christianity; Essays in Honor of H. Shelton Smith*, edited by Stuart Henry (Durham: Duke University Press, 1963), pp. 362–71.

central pulpit with a prayer desk, altar-table, and font all directly in front of it and each progressively lower. The ceiling was painted in imitation of fan vaulting though perfectly flat. The gothic details had a toy-like quality and the building had more in common with Georgian churches than with later gothic revival structures.

Frequent requests for designs led Hopkins to publish his *Essay on Gothic Architecture* in 1836.[10] The plates, done by Hopkins (who had in the meantime become first Bishop of Vermont), illustrate a number of gothic churches. In many of these appear his favorite arrangement—pulpit, desk, altar-table, and font, all on the main axis of the building. Chancels are absent, as are pictures and altar crosses. Hopkins suggested instead "adorning the walls of the Churches only with the appropriate architectural enrichments, and with judicious and edifying selections from the word of God." [11] Hopkins's real attachment to gothic is certainly not for the medieval arrangement but because he felt the "solemnity and repose" of gothic gave a greater "impression of sublimity" than other styles. He chose gothic not because of liturgical requirements but because of its effect upon individual worshipers. Emotive factors here dictate the style.

In a decade or so Hopkins's toy-like gothic had become obsolete. A new orthodoxy reigned and has continued to rule in many denominations up to the present.

The revolution which came to affect thousands of American Protestant churches from the mid-nineteenth century to the present occurred in a most unlikely fashion. More than any other single cause it was the work of a group of undergraduates at Cambridge University in the 1840s banded together as the Cam-

---

[10] *Essay on Gothic Architecture, with Various Plans and Drawings for Churches: Designed Chiefly for the Use of the Clergy* (Burlington, Vermont: Smith and Harrington, 1836).

[11] Ibid. p. 15.

bridge Camden Society.[12] Their professed object was "to promote the study of Ecclesiastical Architecture and Antiquities, and
the restoration of mutilated Architectural remains." Behind such
an innocent program lay some startlingly new ideas. For the real
leaders of the Cambridge Movement, almost without exception,
were men inspired by the theology of the Oxford Movement
with its strong emphasis on the authority of the clergy and the
importance of the sacraments. The Cambridge men were also
convinced that the Middle Ages represented the height of Christian piety and worship and concluded that medieval church
buildings should be reproduced. One of their leaders declared
"that the same shell which contained the apparatus of medieval
worship was, speaking generally, suited to contain that of modern worship." [13] Now this is little short of incredible if one recalls the pains to which the Anglican reformers had gone in
adapting medieval churches for worship according to the *Book
of Common Prayer*.

Nevertheless, the Cambridge Movement prevailed. The writings of John Mason Neale, Benjamin Webb, and others appeared
in numerous pamphlets and in their periodical, the *Ecclesiologist*.
Not only did they succeed in convincing a large segment of the
Church of England that "GOTHICK IS THE ONLY CHRISTIAN ARCHI-
TECTURE," but that the common arrangement for a late medieval
village church was the only acceptable one for Anglicans to use.
Their most important rule was that "every church, of whatever
kind, size, or shape, should have a distinct Chancel *at least* one-
third of the length of the Nave, and separated from the latter,
internally at least, if not externally, by a well-defined mark, a
chancel arch if possible, or at least by a screen and raised

[12] For a detailed account see James F. White, *The Cambridge Movement:
The Ecclesiologists and the Gothic Revival* (Cambridge: Cambridge University Press, 1962).

[13] Beresford Hope, "Mr. Hope's Essay on the Present State of Ecclesiological Science in England," *Ecclesiologist*, VII (1847), 87.

floor." [14] Against the east wall stood the stone altar-table. West-
ward of this were the stalls for choir and clergy. The Cambridge
men fervently advocated a roodscreen for "the separation of the
Clergy from the Laity." In the nave appeared a lectern facing
the congregation, a pulpit on the other side of the chancel arch,
and a font at the western door (Figure 36). It was the entire

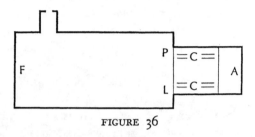

FIGURE 36

medieval arrangement re-introduced in complete reversal of the
auditory tradition prevalent in the Church of England from the
time of Wren. One of the most famous publications of the Cambridge Camden Society was *A Few Words to Churchwardens
on Churches and Church Ornaments: No. 1. Suited to Country
Parishes*,[15] surely one of the most influential publications ever on
church architecture. It contained the full orthodoxy of the Cambridge Movement, ideas which ever since have dominated a large
segment of Protestant church building. The new Coventry Cathedral is only the most recent example of the neo-medieval
arrangement advocated by the Cambridge Camden Society in the
1840s. One only needs to note that in the 1940s an influential
book by an American Methodist advocated the same arrangement to see what a wide circulation these ideas have had.[16]

[14] Editor's note, *Ecclesiologist*, I (1842), 45.

[15] First to thirteenth editions, Cambridge: University Press, 1841 to 1843;
fourteenth edition, London: Joseph Masters, 1846.

[16] Elbert M. Conover, *The Church Builder* (New York: Interdenominational Bureau of Architecture, 1948).

One can sympathize with the Cambridge men in their distaste for the barrenness of churches of their time, particularly those built in one of the classical styles. It is so easily forgotten that most of the furnishings and decorations of Anglican churches today were absent in Anglican churches in the 1840s. The introduction of such items as crosses on bookmarks or candles and crosses on altar-tables could and did cause riots. The Cambridge men boldly championed the introduction of an immense variety of furnishings and decorations copied from medieval patterns.

One of the unfortunate consequences of the Cambridge Movement was in the wholesale adoption of elements of medieval symbolism in arranging and decorating buildings. Thus the rood-screen was justified as signifying the separation of the Church on earth from the Church in heaven. There is a tremendous danger in this type of thought which still plagues church building today. Thinking in symbolic terms can easily obscure functional thought. Far too many churches have adopted items because of a symbolism usually read into them long after their original function had been overlooked. Candles were introduced into churches for the same reason as electric lights and were not commonly placed upon the altar-table until about the twelfth century. Even then the number of candles varied according to need and finances, but two candles have become almost orthodoxy today. Thinking in functional terms often takes one back to earlier traditions than symbolic thought, which usually represents a later development.

Another basic mistake of the Cambridge Movement was in the belief that medieval buildings were suitable for Anglican worship. Yet the whole tradition of Anglican church building since the Reformation had stressed the unity of clergy and laity in offering their worship in such a manner that all was visible and audible. The return to the medieval double rectangle of chancel and nave was a reversal of almost two hundred years of Anglican church building. A very pronounced clericalism is seen in the publications of the Cambridge Movement. It was constantly reiterated that the clergy should sit in chancel and the laity in the nave "exhibiting, what is so wholesome for both to remember, the distinction which must exist between the Clergy and their flocks." [17] Such concepts are far removed from the tendency we see increasing in our times of stressing the positive priesthood of all the faithful. Clericalism is derived from a defective doctrine of the Church which tends to equate the Church with the clergy and to assume that the laity are passive in worship. The neo-medieval arrangement of chancel and nave advocated in the Cambridge Movement seems as foreign to the spirit of the *Book of Common Prayer* as it does to that of the early Church.

A further difficulty arose for which the Cambridge men were not directly responsible. Although at the beginning of the Victorian era churches had small choirs in western galleries, the modern choir dressed in robes and sitting in chancels was not found in parish churches. Such choirs were found in cathedrals where the choir and clergy composed the entire congregation on most occasions. Thus the cathedral service could be both fully choral and congregational. In 1841, Walter Farquhar Hook took the advice of his friend John Jebb and introduced the cathedral form of choral service into his new church in Leeds, placing a choir of laymen in the chancel.[18] This was a radical step in a parish church since it confused the functions of a cathedral and its residential choir with those of a parish church and its congregation. The choir, which was usually the entire congregation in the cathedral and collegiate church, now became an addition to the congregation in the parish church. The consequences are apparent today in many churches: the choir often monopolizes worship almost as much as it would were no other congregation

[17] "On Sedilia and Altar Chairs," *Ecclesiologist*, II (1843), 91.

[18] Cf. John Jebb, *The Choral Service of the United Church of England and Ireland: Being an Enquiry Into the Liturgical System of the Cathedral and Collegiate Foundations of the Anglican Communion* (London: John H. Parker, 1843).

present. The chancels which the Cambridge Movement provided became the natural location for such choirs and ever since they remain physically (if not symbolically) between the congregation and the altar-table.

A further consequence of the Cambridge Movement is the idea that there was only one proper form for a church building, the neo-medieval arrangement with chancel and nave. The publications of the group hammered home the idea that there was such a thing as "correctness" in church building, and experimentation was unnecessary and dangerous. We have seen how many experiments had been conducted to find good liturgical arrangements for Anglican worship before the Cambridge Movement. Since that time, a single pattern has dominated the Anglican communion for over a hundred years. The concept of correctness has led to sterility in church architecture and the discouragement of attempts to break the current stalemate.

The gothic churches built under the influence of the Cambridge Camden Society were usually splendidly decorated. They used abundant stained glass, colored floor tiles, wall paintings, and carved woodwork. This was natural since the leaders of the Movement thought of worship largely in terms of individual response. It was not strange that they should place such importance on the emotive factors of the buildings, for providing an atmosphere was a means of cultivating the aura of awe and mystery that they associated with worship. By contemporary standards their concept of worship seems too subjective and individualistic.

The ideas of the Cambridge Movement were effectively promoted in this country by the New York Ecclesiological Society founded in 1848. The first real landmark was Trinity Church, New York City, finished two years earlier by the architect Richard Upjohn.[19] This building had a deep chancel with a prominent

[19] Cf. Everard M. Upjohn, *Richard Upjohn: Architect and Churchman* (New York: Columbia University Press, 1939), pp. 47–67.

altar. Evidently the depth of the chancel and the cross atop the spire were opposed by the building committee but the architect championed ideas similar to those of the Cambridge men. Its completion, coming only ten years after Bishop Hopkins's book on gothic architecture, shows the rapid changes under way (which Hopkins readily accepted). Trinity has a chancel two bays deep, containing the altar-table with reredos and choir stalls, and immediately beyond are a lectern and pulpit facing the nave.

Such forms became increasingly prevalent in Episcopal churches in nineteenth-century America though not in all. In the years ahead the popularity of gothic was often eclipsed by other styles. Other arrangements appeared too. Trinity Episcopal Church in Boston, consecrated in 1877, was of Romanesque architecture, though planned as no Romanesque church had ever been. Trinity, the church of Phillips Brooks, was designed with the requirements of preaching in mind. A cruciform building, it has galleries in the transepts and accommodates many people close to the preacher. Evidently the chancel was something of an embarrassment for as first designed (by H. H. Richardson) it contained a small altar-table in table form, a D-shaped rail around it, the baptismal font, pulpit and lectern. This arrangement was changed considerably in 1902 and 1938.

The real triumph of the neo-medieval arrangement in Protestant churches dates from what might be called the "second gothic revival." Without much doubt the leading figure in this movement was Ralph Adams Cram (1863–1942).[20] Cram and his associates built a number of churches for most of the major Protestant denominations. An Anglo-Catholic himself, Cram had some reservations about using gothic for Protestants but eventually consented to do so. He emphatically believed that gothic was the style which best expressed the worship of Catholicism. He was scarcely less emphatic in championing the medieval arrange-

[20] Cf. *A Miscellany of American Christianity*, pp. 371–81.

ment of the building. "I need hardly say that the chancel and sanctuary are not only the most sacred portions of a building consecrated to the service of God, but also almost *the* church, the nave being but an adjunct of more or less size provided for the shelter and convenience of worshippers." [21] With Cram's powerful influence, gothic churches with large chancels and the full neo-medieval arrangement became popular among Presbyterians, Congregationalists, Methodists, and Unitarians. Frequently the language was Georgian but the arrangement continued to be medieval. No one seemed troubled by the anomaly of a chancel on a Georgian building built in the twentieth century. The romantic influence of the magnificent Episcopalian cathedrals begun early in this century and the great gothic university chapels erected in the 1920s was felt in Protestant churches all over the land. Every big congregation tried to build a cathedral.

Perhaps even more important than the actual arrangement of these buildings was the subjective concept of worship which informed them. As Cram put it, an important aspect of church architecture is:

the creation of spiritual emotion through the ministry of all possible beauty of environment; the using of art to lift men's minds from secular things to spiritual, that their souls may be brought into harmony with God. . . . Not in the barren and ugly meeting-house of the Puritans . . . were men most easily lifted out of themselves into spiritual communion with God . . . but where they were surrounded by the dim shadows of mysterious aisles . . . where was always . . . the still atmosphere of prayer and praise.[22]

Rapturous language this is indeed, but it is redolent of the same type of individualism one finds in the revivalism Cram abhorred. Cram's effort to provide all manner of means to help men escape

[21] Ralph Adams Cram, *Church Building: A Study of the Principles of Architecture in Their Relation to the Church* (3rd ed.; Boston: Marshall Jones Company, 1924), p. 89.

[22] Ibid. p. 8.

"out of themselves" follows the same subjective concept of worship as one finds in the earlier gothic revival. A modern liturgical scholar criticizes such buildings:

Such edification as it communicates is always individualistic, rarely corporate. For it does not aim to call attention to the action of the liturgy—indeed, it frequently obscures or obstructs the action—but rather to stimulate the contemplation of personal prayer by evocative symbols that surround and adorn, but do not necessarily inhere in the action of the liturgy.[23]

Such subjectivism was a common characteristic of both romanticism and revivalism. Among many twentieth-century Protestants it was expressed as a kind of estheticism. One might be too sophisticated to relish the outward emotionalism of revivalism, but the same stimulation of the feelings might be secured with a "dim religious light" and all the adornments of gothic architecture. In the twentieth century we have seen a great adoption of the neo-medieval arrangement, now referred to as the "divided chancel" among Protestants of every denomination. Very frequently it was couched in gothic terms, otherwise it was likely to appear wearing Georgian clothes. Since World War II it has worn contemporary dress. In any case it is still an arrangement designed primarily for worship by medieval people who were mainly illiterate and could not or would not join in the worship with the clergy.

Von Ogden Vogt and others helped domesticate the gothic revival among Protestants. Vogt, a Unitarian, found, "The intimations of Gothic building, then, are not chiefly intellectual . . . but emotional and mystical."[24] Removed from its association with Catholicism, gothic buildings and all their ornaments were

[23] Massey H. Shepherd, Jr., *The Reform of Liturgical Worship: Perspectives and Prospects* (New York: Oxford University Press, 1961), p. 25.

[24] Von Ogden Vogt, *Art & Religion* (New Haven: Yale University Press, 1921), p. 189. On Vogt see *A Miscellany of American Christianity*, pp. 381–90.

eagerly built by Protestants, before World War II put an end to most building activities.

The gothic style itself was a casualty of the war and the rising building costs thereafter. But the same divided chancel arrangement has remained as one of the two standard Protestant arrangements of our time whether built in pseudo-Georgian or in contemporary idiom. Some indication of how standardized this arrangement has become can be seen in *The Church Builder*, published in 1948 by Elbert M. Conover, director of the Interdenominational Bureau of Architecture. The illustrations alternate between neo-gothic and neo-Georgian, Conover having little patience with "modern." On successive pages appear Congregational, Methodist, Presbyterian, Christian, Lutheran, and Baptist churches each featuring similar divided chancels. No one would have guessed that the Cambridge Movement could have been so successful that its dictums of correctness would be widely imitated by twentieth-century Protestants. It is indeed ironic to read Conover's discussion of a roodscreen, piscina, and sanctuary lamp,[25] and then to reflect upon the reaction of sixteenth-century Protestants to these same items.

III

The contemporary stalemate in Protestant church architecture consists of the uncritical acceptance of two alternate liturgical arrangements as if these were the only possibilities. Actually it is difficult to tell whether the concert stage or the divided chancel arrangement has less to recommend itself for Protestant worship. For the purposes of the present discussion, style is irrelevant since both arrangements have been tried in every possible style. The drawback to the concert stage arrangement is the suggestion that the choir sings to the congregation to stimulate its worship or to

---

[25] *The Church Builder*, pp. 60–64.

exhibit their own skill. No one has ever considered the choir an edifying spectacle to look at even during a long sermon yet this arrangement makes them the dominant visual center of the building. Such an arrangement almost always dwarfs the altar-table and the font or baptistery so that they become insignificant centers buried beneath or behind the pulpit. It also calls excessive attention to the preacher whether he is sitting or standing. The same is true of the organist or choir director, although one gets a view of his back instead.

The divided chancel has other liabilities. The arrangement of a choir on opposite sides of the chancel makes it difficult for them to sing together. After all, this type was invented for antiphonal singing and chanting. The altar-table's being far removed from the congregation suggests a hierarchical concept of the Church which most Protestants do not acknowledge theologically. The remoteness of an altar-table at the end of a chancel makes the action of holy communion seem like a clerical performance. The acts of worship done at the pulpit and lectern tend to seem quite detached from those at the altar-table despite the unity of the visible Word of the sacraments and the preached Word.

The underlying difficulty in both arrangements is that neither is suitable for Protestant concepts of the Church as the whole body of faithful people. In either arrangement the congregation is separated from the clergy and choir by an arbitrary distinction which gives the liturgical centers to the clergy and choir and isolates the congregation from them. The implicit hierarchical distinctions of the longitudinal church would be repudiated by many Protestants if they were put into words, but unconsciously these divisions have been readily accepted.

It may indeed be that our churches are mere reflections of the passivity of modern Protestant congregations with their willingness to let clergy and choir perform the work of common worship for them. Most congregations seem content to seek a worshipful feeling and let the emotive factors of the building and the music waft them into some form of personal devotions. But such a subjective and individualistic approach to worship neglects the importance of worship as the common act of the whole Church. The basic difficulty with the concert stage and the divided chancel arrangements is not simply the practical problems (which would occur to some degree in any type of building) but that they contradict the very nature of the Church itself. These arrangements impede the people's realization of the Church as the body of Christ, and thus interfere with worship, evangelism, and all other aspects of the Church's life.

VI
Recent Experiments

At the present time the Churches of this country are at the beginning of what may be a great new reformation. Indeed historians of subsequent centuries may look back upon our period in time as one of great renewal and strengthening within the Church, just as we now consider the previous century as one of tremendous work in the expansion of the faith. Perhaps no other phrase sums up the various features of the new reformation as does the term "the Liturgical Movement." At its heart are the results of great biblical, theological, historical, and ecumenical stirrings of our time. It is through the Liturgical Movement that this new ferment enters the life of the parish church. It would be impossible to distinguish completely between the Liturgical Movement and the other great movements of our time. The Liturgical Movement tends to be an application and expression of the whole twentieth-century reformation where it most directly affects the life of the Church.

One of the frontiers of theological discussion in our time has been in biblical theology. Some of the main themes are of importance for the Liturgical Movement, particularly the strong stress on the community. Increasingly, we have become aware that the Bible is concerned with the life in faith of an entire people, not just the accounts of individuals. This is equally true of both Old and New Testaments. In the Old Testament we see the relationship of God and man understood through the concept of a covenant which became the charter of a community, God's chosen people. The same images persist in the New Testament in which God in Christ initiates a new covenant. Paul goes so far as to equate being in the life of faith with being in the body of Christ, the Church. We have come to see how central the community is to the Christian life through a greater understanding of the biblical witness on this point.

At the same time it has become apparent how vital worship is in the building up of the community. In Judaism worship re-enacted the great events connected with the origins and preservation of the community, making these same events again present. In a very similar way the early Church was constituted of those who made their offering of worship at the eucharist. Indeed the term "church" may have originally meant the assemblage for worship. Paul speaks of various acts of worship as aiming "at one thing: to build up the church" (I Cor. 14:26). The unity of the church is both expressed and achieved through its sharing bread and wine in doing its worship.

We have also seen in our time some changes in theology regarding worship. There has been a great deal of new interest in the doctrine of the Church. Discussions between Churches in the Ecumenical Movement (the movement concerned with the unity of the Church) have placed the doctrine of the Church in a central position in theological debates. On all hands there seems to be a recognition that a relationship to the Church is a basic characteristic of the Christian life. Furthermore there is a growing emphasis on the nature of the Church as one in which all members have a part and not just the clergy. We see a theology of the laity emerging which stresses the role of the laity in worship, work, and study. The witness of the laity as the Church in the world is seen as a vital part of the Church's ministry.

Exciting theological concepts of worship and its centrality in the Christian life appear in recent books. Dom Odo Casel was a Roman Catholic monk yet his mystery theology is potentially an area of great common interest to Protestants and Catholics.[1] Casel saw worship as largely the re-presentation of the historic events of salvation through the actions of our contemporary worship so that the saving power shown in the past is again made present. We see within Protestantism a rediscovery of the meaning of preaching as an act of worship through which the power of God manifests itself. At the same time, holy communion and baptism have received serious attention among Protestants as much more than signs and symbols.

Many of the new theological developments have been spurred on by historical research. Such research has made it possible for people of all denominations to share in the riches of the whole Christian tradition. Historical studies have led Methodists to realize how far they have moved from eighteenth-century Wesleyanism, Presbyterians to see the gap between themselves and sixteenth-century Calvinists, and other denominations to re-examine their own traditions. Frequently the result has been one of shocked amazement at the differences which separate a denomination from its origin. Often, it seems, the nineteenth century saw the gradual disappearance or disintegration of patterns of worship which once characterized a given tradition. The result in many cases has been a rediscovery of the reformation traditions of each denomination. This has had considerable influence on contemporary thought about worship.

There are dangers in this practice since the Protestant Reformers were limited in their perspectives by the concepts they inherited as children of the late Middle Ages. A more healthy tendency is to do what the Reformers did—appeal to the early

[1] Cf. Dom Odo Casel, *The Mystery of Christian Worship and Other Writings,* edited by Dom Burkhard Neunheuser (Westminster, Md.: Newman, 1962).

Church and Bible. This we can surely do more accurately than they could because of the work of contemporary scholars. Yet even then it is questionable whether we would wish to copy any practices simply because they were primitive.

The value of historic studies of liturgy or liturgical architecture is not in providing examples to copy. This is simply substituting one form of romanticism for another. A fourth-century basilica may be better for modern purposes than a fourteenth-century parish church. But neither is adequate. Rather history helps us to prevent mistakes and also suggests avenues to explore further. It does not answer all our questions but it may help us to raise more significant questions.

The results of biblical, theological, and historical studies can be seen in the Ecumenical Movement. In many cases it has become obvious that the further back we pursue our investigations the more we have common origins. Thus we all ultimately come to our common origin in the Scriptures. It is interesting to see those Roman Catholics who are involved in the Liturgical Movement now advocating items which the Protestant Reformers championed. Celebrating the mass facing the people, using a vernacular language, expecting the people to do their part in the work of worship, all these stem from an appeal to the early Church which we hold as a common tradition. It is interesting to see new Roman Catholic churches being built on patterns long utilized by Protestants but also a bit embarrassing to recognize that some of these churches are more adequate for Protestant worship than many being built today by Protestants.

The Ecumenical Movement has also meant the sharing of many of the elements which used to distinguish denominations. Few denominations care to claim a monopoly on any practices now for all have shared and received from others. It is a bit strange to see Episcopalians in the forefront of those rediscovering speaking in tongues. Some Episcopalians have been a bit startled to realize the necessity of preaching and even the value of praying *extempore* in common worship. Other Protestants have been no less amazed to discover the centrality of the sacraments in the life of the Church. Roman Catholics and Protestants may now be closer in their most profound thinking about worship than in any other area of theological discussion.

The Liturgical Movement has been the arena in which these exciting developments in the thought of the Church have become a part of the life of the Church. Some of the most obvious examples of this new reformation occur in church buildings, often a good index to the life of the Church. It is worth our while to examine a few of the most interesting of these buildings. These are not representative by any means though all suggest possible ideas for future development. Very few of these examples were built before World War II and those presented here represent only a sampling of the interesting buildings recently erected in each tradition. Yet they are hopeful indications that the current stalemate is beginning to be broken and indicate the great possibilities that lie ahead. They should also give encouragement to the cautious since a number of these buildings without any doubt do succeed in expressing the Liturgical Movement in adequate (though not perfect) form. Something can be learned from each example. Many of these buildings can be visited, or seen in the illustrated articles and books cited.

I

Some of the Roman Catholic churches erected in the last few years are of great interest to Protestants for what can be learned from them. It is apparent that Protestants and Catholics now profit from the successes and mistakes of each other's buildings. In a few recent Roman Catholic churches the implications of the Liturgical Movement are clear; many others are as stereotyped as most Protestant churches. Our real concern here is not with how esthetically successful these buildings have been but how well they function as the architectural setting of the mass.

One cannot help being impressed with the concentration on essentials of some Roman Catholic churches erected in Europe since World War II. Though their functions are different, they have in common with the Puritan meetinghouse a rigid exclusion of all that is not essential to common worship. In many cases this has meant that devotional centers—the stations of the cross, images, side altars—have been excluded altogether or relegated to side chapels. Everything in the church focuses one's attention upon the meeting of God and man in the mass. The resulting buildings are austere, deliberately so. But in many cases it cannot be said that they are barren or unattractive. One architect even suggested a white-washed wall behind the altar-table with the priest's vestments and altar-table hangings in strong colors. The wall, after all, is insignificant for the mass; the actions of the priest at the altar-table are central. Too often the wall has been more eye-catching than the altar-table itself. The concentration upon essentials has often resulted in buildings of amazing emotive power too. Frequently this has come about not through a deliberate seeking of beauty but by an honest and sincere effort to make the building function as the best setting for the mass.

Some of the most successful Catholic churches have been built in Germany. Germany and Belgium have been in the forefront of the Liturgical Movement and this is reflected in several churches built in the 1930s which now seem remarkably advanced for their time. They reflect a successful marriage of theology and architecture and have inspired many subsequent buildings.

One of the great German church architects was Dominikus Böhm who died in 1955. Böhm experimented quite successfully with the parabolic arch in the 1920s creating churches with great emotive force. Even more important were his later buildings

which experimented in novel plans. The Church of St. Englebert's in Cologne-Riehl (Figure 37) was consecrated in 1932.² It
is a circular building with the altar-table set in a shallow sanctuary. The building is important as a forerunner of modern circular and elliptical churches, many of which have gone further in
bringing the altar-table out into the midst of the congregation. In

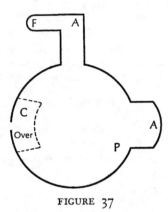

FIGURE 37

St. Englebert's the pulpit is at one side of the entrance to the sanctuary and the baptistery and weekday chapel project from the
circle at right angles to the high altar. At St. Englebert's the
congregation is brought close to the altar-table instead of being
separated from it as in a longitudinal church.

Another great German architect was Rudolf Schwarz (died
in 1961) who designed more than sixty churches. Schwarz spelled
out his principles in church building with profound simplicity:

² For illustrations and floor plans see Peter Hammond, *Liturgy and Architecture* (London: Barrie and Rockliff, 1960), pl. 4 and pp. 58–9; Ferdinand
Pfammatter, *Betonkirchen* (Ensiedeln: Bensiger Verlag, 1948) pl. 20 and 21
and p. 61; Anton Henze and Theodor Filthaut, *Contemporary Church Art*,
translated by Cecily Hastings and edited by Maurice Lavanoux (New York:
Sheed and Ward, 1956), pl. 22 and 23; Joseph Pichard, *Modern Church
Architecture*, translated by Ellen Callmann (New York: Orion, 1962), pl.
17–19.

For the celebration of the Lord's supper a moderately large, well-proportioned room is needed, in its center a table and on the table a bowl of bread and a cup of wine. The table may be decorated with candles and surrounded by seats for the congregation.

That is all. Table, space and walls make up the simplest church.

There have been greater forms of church building than this one but this is not the right time for them. We cannot continue on from where the last cathedrals left off. Instead we must enter into the simple things at the source of the Christian life. We must begin anew and our new beginning must be genuine. The small congregation is given us today, the "coming together of two or three," the communion of the table, and certainly for us the Lord is in the midst of men.[3]

Schwarz's churches reflect this concentration on essentials. His Corpus Christi Church at Aachen (Figure 38) was consecrated in

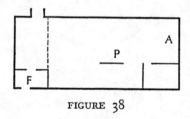

FIGURE 38

1930.[4] It is a rectangular building with no decoration whatsoever, just the altar-table at one end and a pulpit projecting from a wall. There is nothing whatsoever to distract from the mass; everything has been banished but the two main liturgical centers. The baptistery is a separate room. Everything concentrates on the mass without any obvious effort to create a worshipful atmos-

[3] *Vom Bau Der Kirche*, translated as *The Church Incarnate* by Cynthia Harris (Chicago: Henry Regnery, 1958), pp. 35–6.

[4] Cf. Hammond, *Liturgy and Architecture*, pp. 56–7; Pfammatter, *Beton-kirchen*, pl. 23, p. 73; *Towards a Church Architecture*, edited by Peter Hammond (London: Architectural Press, 1962), pp. 129–31.

phere. Yet the building is one of very great beauty because of the honest use of materials and fine proportions.

Schwarz was responsible for a number of churches built during the rebuilding of Germany since World War II. One of the most interesting of these is St. Michael's Church in Frankfort (Figure 39) built in 1954.[5] The building is basically an ellipse with the

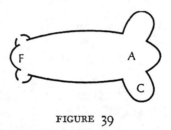

FIGURE 39

altar-table near one focus. However, rooms have been added on either side of the ellipse both facing the main altar-table. One accommodates the choir, the other serves as a weekday chapel with devotional centers. The font is at the opposite end of the building. St. Michael's is one of a number of new buildings which are experiments with the ellipse or even more complicated forms of distorted ellipses as well as trapezoids, hexagons, etc. The attempt has been to shape the building to the requirements of the liturgy.

The flowering of the Liturgical Movement in French Catholicism has been slower, but since World War II it has blossomed. The role of the Church as a minority group in its impact upon the masses has led to a return to essentials rarely accomplished when the Church appears successful. Out of this have

[5] Illustrated in Albert Christ-Janer and Mary Mix Foley, *Modern Church Architecture: A Guide to the Form and Spirit of 20th Century Religious Buildings* (New York: McGraw-Hill Book Company, 1962), pp. 67–9; *Church Buildings Today* (now *Churchbuilding*), #5 (1962), 17–18; *Towards a Church Architecture*, p. 144; Pichard, *Modern Church Architecture*, pl. 59.

come some fundamental changes in thinking about worship and mission. This is reflected architecturally in many new churches in France as a fascination with "poverty," the term being used in the sense of restraint. Rainer Senn is a young Swiss architect who has built a number of churches in France. He writes, *"The limitation of financial means generally has a positive effect on the appearance of a building* . . . for in this way the architect learns the 'discipline of conditions of privation': to examine thoroughly the requirements of a building in order to find fundamentals." [6] Senn goes on to say, "My aim has been that each individual should be aware on the one hand of *his togetherness with others* and on the other hand of *his relationship to a common centre.*"

Senn has designed several churches in France at extraordinary low costs. His Church of Our Lady of Lourdes at Pontarlier, France, built in 1959 (Figure 40), is a remarkable building.[7] The

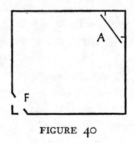

FIGURE 40

plan resembles somewhat the Akron plan except there is no pulpit. The altar-table is in the corner of a square building and the congregation faces it in two sections of seating at right angles to each other. The liturgical space about the altar-table is defined

[6] Rainer Senn, "The Spirit of Poverty," *Churchbuilding*, #9 (1963), 23. *L'Art Sacré* devotes the issue of Jan.-Feb. 1958 to "La transparence de la pauvreté."

[7] Peter Hammond, "Modern Churches in Postwar France," *Architectural Record*, CXXVII (June, 1960), pp. 210-11; *Towards a Church Architecture*, pp. 164-6; *L'Art Sacré* (July-Aug. 1958), 6-11.

by light from a large window in the roof which lights the sanctuary without shining in the face of the congregation. A central
diagonal aisle leads from the font at the entrance to the altar-
table. The building is utter simplicity and yet it has all the essentials for Catholic worship.

In Grenoble, France, the Church of St. Jacques (Figure 41)

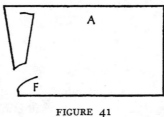

FIGURE 41

was completed in 1959 under the direction of the firm of Vin-
cent, Pupat, and Potié.[8] This is a simple wooden rectangle. The
free-standing altar-table is set in the middle of one long side. Pews
surround the altar-table on three sides. Thus the plan is basically
that of the Puritan meetinghouse type common in America
1700–70 with the altar-table the dominant liturgical center instead of the pulpit. Overhead is a large skylight which admits a
burst of light on the altar-table.

In this country a number of experiments have also been made
by Roman Catholics. One of the earlier examples is St. Mark's
Church, Burlington, Vt. (Figure 42), designed by the firm of
Freeman, French, and Freeman.[9] St. Mark's is in the form of a
Greek cross. The altar-table stands in the center of the building
surrounded by rails on four sides. Three arms of the cross provide seating for the congregation with a door at each end. The

[8] Peter Hammond, "Modern Churches in Postwar France," *Architectural
Record*, CXXVII (June 1960), 213.

[9] "St. Mark's Church, Burlington, Vermont," *Architectural Forum*, LXXXI
(July 1944), 85–90.

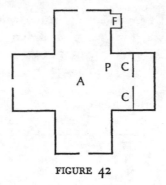

FIGURE 42

fourth side contains the choir stalls and pulpit and (behind a screen) sacristy. Clerestory windows (over a lower part of the roof) above the central sanctuary give additional light.

The ultimate development in the central church is seen in the octagonal Church of the Blessed Sacrament, built in Holyoke, Mass. (Figure 43), under the direction of architect Chester F.

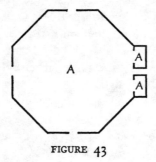

FIGURE 43

Wright.[10] Eight rows of pews surround the altar-table. Thus a large congregation is brought close to the central liturgical center. The cross suspended over the altar-table has a corpus on either side. Clerestory windows illuminate the central space.

[10] "Church in the Round," *Architectural Forum*, IC (Dec. 1953), 101.

These Catholic churches have a number of common factors despite their apparent dissimilarities. In a number of new Catholic churches the altar-table is definitely table-like in form despite the explicit criticism of this in a papal encyclical.[11] Frequently liturgical space about the altar-table is made to stand out by the use of lighting from above or at the sides, a feature common in baroque churches. The problem of where to place the tabernacle if one is to celebrate from behind the main altar-table has led to some experiments. In the Church of St. Sebastian in Aachen (designed by Lieter) the tabernacle is held in a free-standing arch behind the altar-table. A special table with a baldachino over it was provided for the tabernacle in Schwarz's adaptation of the medieval Church of Our Lady, Trier.[12] There has also been a tendency to have only one altar-table in the church or to remove side altar-tables to distinct chapels.

In many recent experiments the tendency has been to adopt a central type of building with the deliberate intention of bringing the people as close to the altar-table as possible. This has led to the use of a tremendous variety of forms, including egg-shape, fan-shape, and all manner of ellipses, circles, octagons, etc. Some concern has been shown about making the congregation space more flexible so that processions are possible and the people do not feel regimented by rows of pews.[13] In most recent churches the baptistery has been separated from the main space of the building, often being placed in such a way as to emphasize baptism as the sacrament which brings one into the Church. Many of these Catholic experiments in liturgical architecture are of

[11] *Christian Worship: Encyclical Letter (Mediator Dei) of His Holiness Pius XII* (London: Catholic Truth Society, 1947), section 66.

[12] Henze and Filthaut, *Contemporary Church Art*, pl. 40 and 41.

[13] H. A. Reinhold, *Speaking of Liturgical Architecture* (Notre Dame: Liturgical Programs, University of Notre Dame, 1952), pp. 18–21. Cf. page 21 for an interesting plan realized in St. Joseph's Church, Sunnyside, Wash., in 1950.

interest to Protestants because of their purposes and the means by which these have been accomplished.

II

The period since World War II has seen a great number of experiments among Protestants with regard to liturgical architecture. The problem for Protestants of many traditions has been more complex than for Roman Catholics. Roman Catholic churches need not have an impressive pulpit; St. Michael's in Frankfort has none at all. But the Protestant needs to make both pulpit and altar-table significant without either one making the other appear inconsequential. At the same time the font cannot be obscured. It is interesting to watch attempts to solve this problem in the Reformed tradition which places a high value on preaching and yet is in the process of rediscovering the importance of the visible Word of the sacraments.

In the Reformed Church at Zürich-Alstetten (Figure 44), de-

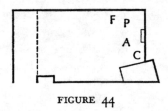

FIGURE 44

signed by Werner Moser in 1941, an interesting solution was used.[14] At the east end a small platform reaches across the front upon which appears a large cross standing upon the floor. On one side of it is the pulpit before which stands the font; on the other side appear the altar-table, the choir, and organ. The spreading

[14] Peter Hammond, *Liturgy and Architecture*, p. 65; Christ-Janer and Foley, *Modern Church Architecture*, pp. 222–9; and Pfammatter, *Betonkirchen*, pl. 53–6 and p. 100.

arms of the cross and a large wall panel with the words, "One is our Master, Christ, and we are all brothers," link the liturgical centers. The solution is that of balancing pulpit and altar-table yet tying them together. The skill with which this has been done in this particular instance keeps the two liturgical centers from competing with each other and gives them visual unity.

Some of the most interesting experiments in the Reformed tradition have been tried in the Dutch Reformed Church as war-destroyed churches are rebuilt and new ones erected in housing estates. In some of these there has been an awareness of the possibilities explored in the first Protestant churches built in the Netherlands, yet there is no slavish copying of them. Such an instance is the Maranatha Church of Amsterdam-Zuid (Figure 45)

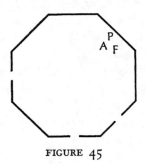

FIGURE 45

built in 1954, J. H. Groenewegen and H. Mieras working with G. J. Rutgers, architects.[15] The building is octagonal like some seventeenth-century Dutch churches. It also has a large sounding board over the pulpit in the same tradition. History has been used to inform the present but not to dictate to it in the building. The pulpit stands against one wall, with the altar-table and font side by side on a small platform in front of it. Pews along the two

[15] *Ark: 10 Jaar Kerkbouw*, a special number of *Forum*, XII (March 1957), 10–15.

adjacent walls and in the central space face the liturgical centers grouped thus tightly together.

An interesting experiment has been tried in the Advent Church (Figure 46) in the Hague.[16] Designed in 1955 by the firm of

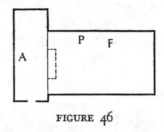

FIGURE 46

Zanstra, Giesen and Sijmons with the aid of K. L. Sijmons, it is a rectangle with the pulpit in the center of one of the long sides, again a familiar Dutch position. Below and to one side of it is the font. The most interesting change is a separate room for the eucharist below the organ gallery and opening off one of the short ends of the room at right angles to the axis on which the pulpit appears. In the eucharist room a long table and chair for the minister normally stand. Possibly other tables and benches are added at time of communion so the people can gather about them to receive communion sitting. The rest of the time the room is visible but evidently not used.

It would seem that there are advantages to this arrangement in giving clear liturgical space to the different acts of worship just as in English churches where the chancel was long used as the communion room and the nave for the daily offices and preaching. There is a problem though in obscuring the fact that the Word preached and the Word visible are the same. This problem is particularly acute in Protestant groups which have tended to ignore the sacraments and to forget that the sacraments too proclaim the Gospel. It may be necessary for some time to stress the

[16] Ibid. pp. 5–9.

unity of sermon and sacrament in many denominations. The same is true, of course, of those groups which have tended to slight the Word made manifest in preaching.

Several Dutch churches reveal fresh attempts to unite the three main liturgical centers in a meaningful fashion. In the Redeemer Church of Bussum (Nielsen, Spruit and Van der Kuilen architects, 1956) an elliptical building has been used (Figure 47).[17] At

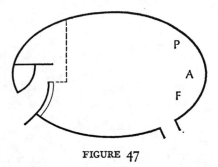

FIGURE 47

one of the sharper ends is a small platform with an altar-table and minister's chair at its center. On one side is a pulpit, at the other the font. The font has been given an excellent spatial treatment by being enclosed by a rail. Some rather original approaches appear in the Resurrection Church in Amsterdam-West (Figure 48), designed by M. F. Duintjer and erected in 1956.[18] The build-

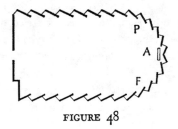

FIGURE 48

[17] Ibid. pp. 16–21.
[18] Ibid. pp. 22–7.

ing is basically a rectangle rounded off at one end. The platform at the east end contains a very large wooden cross. Directly beneath it is an altar-table with four benches, one on each side. At one side is the pulpit and on the other appears the font, carved from a large boulder.

One of the most successful of the new Dutch churches is the Cross Church of Amstelveen (Figure 49) designed by M. F.

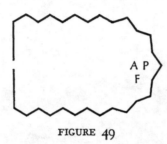

A P
F

FIGURE 49

Duintjer in 1951.[19] In this building the altar-table is directly in front of the pulpit both being on the main axis of a building basically rectangular with one end rounded. Over the pulpit is a large sounding board which extends forward to become a baldachino over the altar-table. Thus both liturgical centers are united very effectively. To one side appears the font. In the Christian Reformed Maranatha Church in Eindhoven (A. Nicolai, architect, 1953) font, altar-table, and pulpit are in one line projecting into the nave and surrounded on three sides by the congregation.

The variety seen within the Dutch Reformed Church is amazing, yet there are some common factors. In almost every case the altar-table is built like a long table and is used as a table, the people sitting around it to receive the Lord's supper. The minister's chair which appears behind it in a number of cases is evidently not meant to echo the bishop's chair in the early basilica since the pulpit is used for preaching and the chair is used during

[19] *Kerk en Kunst*, VIII (1953–54), pl. 2 and 3.

the Lord's supper, probably precisely at those times when it would not have been used in the early Church. The pulpits express very well the authority and dignity of the preached Word. This is especially true of the sounding boards, a traditional item in the Netherlands yet treated in a contemporary fashion. Some of these are very forceful statements of a theology of proclamation.[20]

In many cases an attempt has been made to place the congregation as close as possible to the liturgical centers. This has resulted in the use of a variety of unusual forms, ellipses, cross forms, octagons, etc. Some of these come from the Dutch tradition, but traditional forms have been used in original ways to guide further experiments.[21] The new Dutch churches have shown some very imaginative means of placing pipe organs so that the pipes become interesting features of the building without being obtrusive.

III

The situation in the Church of England has been quite different. Here we see a massive conservatism which only in the last few years has shown any signs of crumbling. The power of the Cambridge Movement is still very much present in the Church of England just as among many American Protestant denominations. Church groups go on building according to the same neo-medieval plan with the choir intervening between the congregation and the altar-table. In a sense the new Coventry Cathedral is probably the last great nineteenth-century church. Despite its artistic éclat, the building is basically a romantic structure striving for (and accomplishing very well) the creation of a mood. It reflects nineteenth-century concepts of worship, not those of the

[20] Cf. the Dutch Reformed Church of Oosterbeek, Ibid. plates 8a and 9; *Architectural Record*, CXIV (Dec. 1953), 122.

[21] Cf. comparative chart of these, *Kerk en Kunst*, VIII (1953–54), opposite p. 716.

modern Liturgical Movement. It is interesting to contrast Coventry as built with one of the rejected designs. The design of Alison and Peter Smithson [22] would have been a square building with the altar-table standing on the diagonal axis half-way toward the center of the building. The choir stalls, organ, pulpit and lectern would have been part of a raised gallery which would have allowed a direct view of the altar-table from the sides and front while at the same time defining the space about it.

In recent years the Liturgical Movement has made considerable progress in England. The old practices of holy communion as an early service attended by a few devout souls or a high mass at which no one but the clergy communicated have been superseded in many areas by the parish communion. The parish communion is meant to be the normal weekly assembly for worship of the parish with the laity receiving communion.[23] Increased emphasis is placed on the laity's participating directly in reading the lessons, in the offertory procession, and hymn singing. There have been some interesting consequences as it is realized that the neo-medieval double rectangle of chancel and nave impedes congregational participation.

One of the earliest churches to show the effects of the parish communion movement was the John Keble Church, Mill Hill in London (Figure 50), designed by D. F. Martin-Smith in 1936.[24] It was one of the first in England, if not the first, to break away from the neo-medieval arrangement. Here is a rectangular nave with the choir and clergy stalls projecting into one of the long sides in a fashion reminiscent of the basilican arrangement. The

[22] "Design for Coventry Cathedral 1951," *Churchbuilding*, #8 (Jan. 1963), 4–17.

[23] Cf. *The Parish Communion; A Book of Essays*, edited by A. G. Hebert (London: S.P.C.K., 1937); also *The Parish Communion Today: The Report of the 1962 Conference of Parish and People*, edited by David M. Paton (London: S.P.C.K., 1962).

[24] Cf. Peter Hammond, *Liturgy and Architecture*, pl. 28 and pp. 72–3.

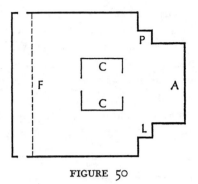

FIGURE 50

altar-table, however, is in a shallow sanctuary beyond the stalls and stands against the wall. The congregation sits on three sides of the choir and are all close to the altar-table. The minister must still celebrate with his back to the congregation in this church. Movable chairs give the congregation greater flexibility. The pulpit and lectern stand at the corners of the sanctuary and nave. This church represents a cautious use of the basilican arrangement. Elsewhere it has had fuller use.

Since World War II there have been an increasing number of English churches which express the conjunction of the Liturgical Movement and contemporary architecture. The Church of the Ascension, Crownhill, Plymouth (Figure 51) designed by Robert Potter and Richard Hare, 1958, is a cruciform building with

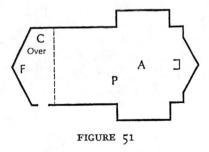

FIGURE 51

shallow arms.[25] The altar-table stands in the crossing with the congregation sitting in the transepts and nave. The choir and organ are in a rear gallery. Over the altar-table is a baldachino and rails surround it on three sides. Seats for the clergy and a combination lectern-pulpit stand before the altar-table and a bishop's chair behind it.

One of the most interesting new buildings is St. Paul, Bow Common, London (Figure 52) built according to the designs of

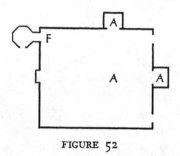

FIGURE 52

Robert Maguire and Keith Murray in 1960.[26] The building is almost square. The altar-table is located toward the center of the building. Its liturgical space has been defined by a change in the level and paving of the floor as well as by lighting fixtures which encircle the space. There are no rails. Above the altar-table are a baldachino and clerestory windows. One enters the church through an octagonal porch passing the large font. There is processional space well defined about the perimeter of the building. Two small chapels open off the main space.

Other new churches in England follow a variety of forms though the English have always been a bit reluctant about curved shapes. Most of these new experiments have free-standing altar-tables so that the minister can celebrate from behind and face the

[25] Ibid. pl. 34 and pp. 118–19.

[26] Ibid. pp. 111–14, and *Towards a Church Architecture*, pp. 154–8.

congregation. Frequently there is only one altar-table in the church, avoiding the implicit divisiveness of several. In some cases the buildings are centrally planned, squares, Greek crosses, octagons, etc. Often the font is placed near the altar-table and pulpit.[27]

The year 1960 may well mark a great turning point in English church architecture. That year saw the publication of Peter Hammond's book, *Liturgy and Architecture*, which may well be the most significant book on the subject since the Cambridge Camden Society's *A Few Words to Churchwardens* (1841). Hammond is not a bit more subtle than John Mason Neale though his concepts of liturgical architecture are very different. *Liturgy and Architecture* flays the timidity of English church builders and gives examples of exciting buildings on the Continent and a comparatively small number in England. The last few years have seen the activity of the New Churches Research Group with a few mimeographed publications and a number of articles in the excellent periodical, *Churchbuilding*.[28] Some of the papers read at the New Churches Research Group conferences have been published in *Towards a Church Architecture*. Recently an Institute for the Study of Worship and Religious Architecture has been established at the University of Birmingham.[29] With such distinguished groups working on liturgical architecture there is

[27] J. G. Davies, *The Architectural Setting of Baptism* (London: Barrie and Rockliff, 1962), p. 153.

[28] The New Churches Research Group is composed of members of various denominations, many of whom are architects. The Honorary Secretary is Dr. Patrick Nuttgens of the Institute of Advanced Architectural Studies, University of York, Micklegate, York. *Churchbuilding* is published by John Catt Limited, 116a High Street, Billericay, Essex. It appears three times a year and costs $2.50 mailed to this country. *Your Church*, a bimonthly published by the Religious Publishing Company, 122 Old York Road, Jenkintown, Pa., is the nearest American equivalent. It costs $1.75 a year.

[29] The Director is Professor J. G. Davies, University of Birmingham, Birmingham, England.

great hope for some significant buildings in the future. Unfortunately we have no similar research group or place of study in this country.

An additional concern has been shown in recent years in adapting older churches for contemporary concepts of worship. The process in England is referred to as "re-ordering." The problem is stated succinctly by Bishop J. A. T. Robinson:

> A very ordinary, traditionalist and entirely uncranky vicar, with a barn of a Victorian-Gothic church, said to me recently, "I shall never begin to get my people to see themselves as the Body of Christ until the entire lay-out of this building has been changed." I am sure he was right; but until a year or two ago few would have seen the first problem in evangelism to be architecture. . . . The church building is a prime aid, or a prime hindrance, to the building up of the Body of Christ. And what the building says so often shouts something entirely contrary to all that we are seeking to express through the liturgy. And the building will always win—unless and until we can make it say something else.[30]

It is a problem relevant to many who have inherited churches in this country built according to the neo-medieval plan. Gilbert Cope has edited a symposium entitled *Making the Building Serve the Liturgy: Studies in the Re-ordering of Churches.* In it he writes, "Nowadays it is recognized that there could be no greater architectural obstacle to the realization of Christian community in worship than the romantic imposition of the medieval *cathedral* pattern on the design of a parish church." [31]

Examples of such buildings appear with suggestions for their re-ordering.[32] In the medieval Abbey Church at Shrewsbury, a building with a nave, shallow transepts, choir in the crossing, and

[30] *Making the Building Serve the Liturgy: Studies in the Re-ordering of Churches,* edited by Gilbert Cope (London: A. R. Mowbray, 1962), p. 5.

[31] Ibid. p. 36.

[32] Ibid. pp. 64–6.

remote sanctuary, the suggested re-ordering is interesting. It was recommended that the high altar-table be located where the choir now is, the choir to sit in the present sanctuary. People could sit in the south transept. Two altar-tables would be eliminated, one secondary altar-table remaining in a side chapel. The font would be moved to a more conspicuous position at the west end. Structurally the building would not be changed but the re-ordering of its contents would help it express its functions better. Moving liturgical centers and the creation of new liturgical spaces would help make this ancient building appropriate for contemporary worship.

IV

Until quite recently the vast majority of Protestant churches built in this country derived from one or the other of the two types described in Chapter V. Indeed most churches being built today reflect the same stalemate. But there have been a few churches built since World War II which show signs of recent thought about the basic requirements for Protestant worship and the number of these buildings seems to be increasing slowly but steadily.

The situation has been complicated in America by the well-known practice in many denominations of "aping the Anglicans" on the assumption that Episcopalians knew what they were doing in building "correct" neo-medieval churches. As shown in the previous chapter, this type of arrangement is a dubious blessing, to say the least. Yet Episcopalians continue to build it and other Protestants to imitate them. Given this situation, it is perhaps only just to say that some Episcopalians have also been the first to revolt against the tyranny of the divided chancel.

The Episcopal Church of Saint Clement, Alexandria, Va. (Figure 53) designed by Joseph H. Saunders in 1949 may well mark

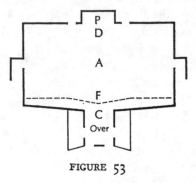

FIGURE 53

the turning point.[33] The rector, Darby Betts, discussed for some time the centrality of the altar-table until a vestryman exclaimed, "Well, why don't we put it in the center!" Encouraged by the example of St. Mark's Roman Catholic Church, they did exactly this. The altar-table is at the center of a rectangular building, the congregation in two groups opposite either end. The main entrance is in the center of an arm projecting from one of the long sides and one passes the font upon entering. The altar-table faces the main entrance and has a cross suspended over it and rails on all four sides. Behind the altar-table in a slight recess in the wall stand the reading desk and pulpit in a double-decker arrangement reminiscent of eighteenth-century pulpits. The choir sits over the main entrance. The building has no windows and this may be a disadvantage for it might suggest that worship is irrelevant to daily life. St. Clement's was perhaps the first experiment with a central altar-table in modern American Protestantism. In it a very deliberate attempt was made to enable the congregation to understand itself as the family of God gathered about the Lord's

---

[33] Cf. *Architectural Forum*, XCI (Dec. 1949), 63; Paul Thiry, Richard M. Bennett, and Henry L. Kamphoefner, *Churches and Temples* (New York: Reinhold, 1953), pp. 54p–55p; Katherine M. McClinton, *The Changing Church: Its Architecture, Art, and Decoration* (New York: Morehouse-Gorham, 1957), p. 73.

table. The pulpit and font too are in the midst of the congregation.

A subsequent experiment was tried in a summer chapel, the Chapel of St. James the Fisherman (Figure 54) at Wellfleet on

FIGURE 54

Cape Cod.[34] Designed by Olaf Hammarstrom in 1956, the building is a square structure with the altar-table at the center. The congregation is arranged in four segments on the diagonals of the building, the aisles being on the two main axes. In the aisle on one side of the altar-table is the pulpit and on the opposite side the font. An octagonal rail encloses the altar-table. The clergy sit with their family (as in eighteenth-century churches) and the choir, too, sits with the rest of the congregation. Although the building seats 320 people, no one is more than six seats from the main liturgical center. Laymen read the lessons standing at their seats in the congregation. The arrangement enables the congregation to take an active part in the service.

Subsequent experiments have utilized the central altar-table. In St. Luke's Episcopal Church in Dallas, Tex. (Figure 55), built in 1959 (William Hidell, architect) the altar-table is near the center of the building with a rail all the way around.[35] Nine rows of pews

[34] Cf. Christ-Janer and Foley, *Modern Church Architecture*, pp. 163-70.

[35] Cf. *The Episcopalian*, CXXVI (May 1961), 28-9.

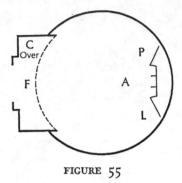

FIGURE 55

encircle the altar-table about two-thirds of the way around the building. Behind the altar-table is the bishop's throne, on either side of which appear the lectern and pulpit. The choir is in a gallery over the main entrance, the font below it. The same thing has been accomplished in a rather different way in the Episcopal Church of the Good Shepherd, built in Lyndhurst, O. (Figure 56) according to the designs of Hays and Ruth (1958). This

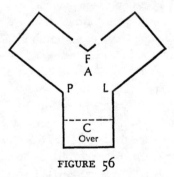

FIGURE 56

building is shaped like a "Y," the altar-table being in the center and pulpit, lectern, and font at the intersections of the three arms in which the congregation sits. Choir and organ are in a gallery over one of the wings.

The building with the altar-table in the exact center poses a number of problems. Professor Massey H. Shepherd, Jr. has pointed out the disadvantages of an altar-table in the dead center of the building: the minister's inability to face those behind him, the "difficulty of the congregation acting together as one body," and the inability to distinguish the various ministries within one body.[36] Shepherd does not condemn by any means a free standing altar-table or a central type of plan, but he insists that the altar-table in the exact center has been tried and rejected repeatedly throughout the history of the Church.

A more satisfactory solution seems to have been found in St. Bede's Church, Menlo Park, Calif. (Figure 57) designed by John

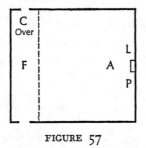

FIGURE 57

Hill in 1962. The building is square. The altar-table stands a short distance from the center of one wall. It is encircled by rails on four sides and pews on three sides. Behind it and against the wall are lectern, credence table, and pulpit. The choir is in a gallery at the rear with the font below. There is a hanging cross over the altar-table which is a good example of table-form. The building has a very real sense of intimacy between the people and the liturgical centers. Indeed the congregation obviously occupies much of the liturgical space of the building.

[36] Massey H. Shepherd, Jr., "Central Sanctuary—A Fallacy in Design," *The Witness*, XLIX (Feb. 9, 1961), 10–13.

Other denominations have on occasions shown vigorous interest in experimentation. St. John's Lutheran Church, Midland, Mich. (Figure 58) was built in 1955 according to the designs of

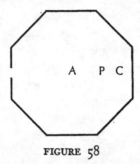

FIGURE 58

Alden B. Dow. It is an octagon with the altar-table at the center. The congregation is arranged on seven sides of the altar-table with the pulpit and choir occupying the eighth side. Above the altar-table is a very dramatic skylight. One of the disadvantages of the central position is reflected in the altar-table which is octagonal in this case and suggests neither an altar nor a table.

A hexagon building was designed in 1963 by Morrell H. Shoemaker for the Englewood Methodist Church in Chicago (Figure 59). Here the altar-table is in the center with the lectern between

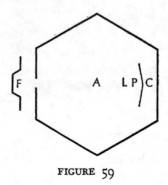

FIGURE 59

it and the pulpit. Pews parallel to the walls surround the altar-table on five sides. The choir is ranged along the sixth wall and directly in front of the choir is the pulpit. The font is in a recess in the opposite wall near the main entrance. Rails surround the altar-table on six sides. In the St. Andrew's Methodist Church, Dallas, Tex., the present church (designed by Braden and Jones in 1962) is a hexagon. The altar-table is in the center with the congregation on five sides. Behind on one side is the pulpit and on the other side the font. A screen encloses the open space behind these for a sacristy.

A more unusual use of a hexagon, this time with two parallel sides elongated, appears in Bethany Presbyterian Church in Portland, Ore.[37] This building was designed by John F. Jensen and Louis C. Gilham (Figure 60). In this church the altar-table is run

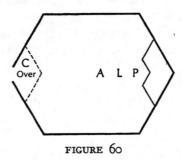

FIGURE 60

table-wise, that is, parallel to the long walls, and stands in the center of the building. The congregational space is U-shaped around the platform on which stands the altar-table. At the end with no seating is the pulpit and directly in front of it a lectern. The altar-table running lengthwise was once common in Presbyterian churches in Scotland. This church seats 250 people, none

[37] Cf. "The Church Around the Table," *Presbyterian Life*, XI (Oct. 15, 1958), 15–16; and "This Congregation Sits About the Table," *Protestant Church Administration and Equipment*, VII (Feb. 1959), 8–9.

of them more than twenty feet from the altar-table. Perhaps because of this new arrangement the congregation has welcomed
more frequent communion services. The choir is in a gallery at
the rear.

It should be pointed out that none of these buildings is spec-
tacular, structurally or esthetically, with the possible exception of
St. John's Lutheran. Yet these congregations have taken the risk
of conducting experiments to find more adequate settings for
Protestant worship. Everyone should be able to profit from their
achievements and mistakes. None is perfect but certainly more
adequate than a divided chancel or concert stage arrangement,
as their congregations and pastors have often testified.

The diversities between these buildings are numerous but one
can soon see how many common factors there are and how these
cut across denominational lines. In several instances the altar-table
has the shape of a table. One notices a tendency to increase the
prominence of the font and to give it distinct space. No doubt the
size of the font in many Protestant churches is an index of how
casually the sacrament of baptism has often been treated. Perhaps
the new fonts are a sign that this has been reversed. Several new
churches indicate a tendency to reduce the number of liturgical
centers, particularly by eliminating the lectern. At the same time
the pulpit may become more prominent.

Many congregations have had the advantage of worshiping in
school auditoriums or gymnasiums before erecting their own
building. This has given an opportunity for experimentation at no
cost, for it is possible in these circumstances to arrange chairs,
tables, and lecterns in all manner of positions. One can try out an
arrangement without being committed to it by a building. The
benefits of this have been reflected in a number of new buildings.

Many of these new churches strongly emphasize that congregational space is also liturgical space, not just the seating of spectators. The use of central plans puts the congregation close to the
liturgical centers even though these are not necessarily in the

center of the building. The congregation has more direct access to the liturgical centers. In denominations where the communicants kneel about a rail, the rails now frequently encircle the altar-table. It goes without saying that the length of these services is inversely proportional to the length of the rail. Some churches have discovered that the rail can be dispensed with provided there is a step for kneeling. The other liturgical centers—a font or baptistery and pulpit—are often given a position in the midst of the congregation to help the people appropriate for their own the work performed at them. Certainly the new emphasis is on churches where all the people of God can actively perform their work of worship rather than be mere spectators.

V

It is tempting to speculate upon what new experiments will be tried in the near future and what approaches may come to prevail in the next few years. One thing can be sure, it is not likely that we will see types as stereotyped as the two patterns that still flourish. It would be disastrous if any concept of a "correct" arrangement should emerge as it did in the case of the Cambridge Movement. This is unlikely so long as a healthy dialogue between architecture and theology continues. It is only when this becomes a monologue that sterility is a danger.

It may well be that there will be some common features in the experiments of the future. A tendency to build the altar-table in a table-like form is already discernible. This might be best done if the table form were to persist but the material be stone, since the concept of sacrifice (often associated with this material) will probably be treated with more seriousness by Protestants in the future.[38] Perhaps an ideal form would be a horizontal slab supported by a vertical slab in the middle. This would allow the min-

[38] Cf. Gustaf Aulén, *Eucharist and Sacrifice*, translated by Eric Wahlstrom. (Edinburgh: Oliver and Boyd, 1958).

ister to conduct the service from behind it without his legs being a distraction. At the same time, the form of a table would be apparent. Altar rails may become less common in the future since they are not really necessary for kneeling.

No doubt we will see more prominent fonts, often of stone. In many cases they may be given adequate spatial treatment. Some congregations may wish to retain the ancient symbolism of the font placed a step or two below the pavement so that those being baptized show forth their descending and rising from the grave with Christ. Though many fonts will be placed at the entrance to the church, it is possible that some will be located in a wide spot in the central aisle or at some other point where one approaches the altar-table space. This will have the advantage of making baptism an act of worship of the entire congregation but will also indicate that baptism is an act of entrance into the fellowship which gathers for the holy communion.

The pulpit, no doubt, will retain its significant size and in many cases may absorb the function of the lectern. Perhaps a sense of majesty and authority will be increased by the use of massive dimensions, stone or other sturdy materials, and sounding boards. The pulpit will be related to the altar-table to stress the unity of the Word preached and the Word made visible in the sacrament and neither liturgical center will compete too vigorously with the other for visual attention.

It is quite possible that pulpit, font, and altar-table will be the only liturgical centers in many Protestant churches. Very likely the unity of these centers will be shown in various ways: similarity in texture, materials, and decoration, by the use of color, by changes in the color or level of the floor or roof, or by lighting fixtures. Possibly the use of sounding boards and baldachinos will be exploited for their full artistic and dramatic possibilities. These can stress the unity of the various works of worship.

At the same time there will remain the need to allow adequate and distinct liturgical space for the use of each of these liturgical centers. This has often been neglected in the case of baptism which tends to lose some of its distinctive nature when the font is placed immediately adjacent to the altar-table. The skillful use of liturgical spaces will express the distinctiveness of the acts performed in them while the design of the centers may signify their essential unity.

It is very probable that we will see increasing numbers of centrally-planned churches. This is not to say that the liturgical centers will necessarily be in the exact center of the building since that leads to further difficulties, especially when the congregation surrounds the altar-table or pulpit. But more attention will be given to placing the congregation in as close proximity to the liturgical centers as possible. Probably the present-day experiments which have placed the congregation in transepts or other separated areas will be little imitated. Such arrangements make preaching very difficult. They also foster the illusion of two or more separate congregations instead of one body gathered about the Lord's table. The basic problem of the central church plan then is to gather the congregation about the altar-table, pulpit, and font without fragmenting it. This will require considerable further experimentation though some of the examples mentioned in this chapter can be helpful in pointing the direction.

It is to be expected that we will see more concrete realization of the fact that the space which the congregation occupies is liturgical space as much as that occupied by the clergy. Most likely the audience hall type of long naves, sloping floors, and comfortable pews will be rare in the future. It is quite possible that galleries will be little used. With the liturgical centers as close as possible to the congregation, the people will have easier access to them and the notion of certain places in the church as holy spots, monopolized by the clergy and choir, will be lessened considerably. The impression that God is out beyond the east window will be avoided by centrally planned buildings.

It is even possible, though perhaps one cannot hope for so

much, that the rigid regimentation of immovable banks of pews will be replaced with chairs that are movable. After all, there is no canon that a congregation has to be arrayed in ranks like soldiers lined up for inspection on either side of a central aisle. Instead it should be possible to widen an aisle at one spot to place a font or to place seating closer about an altar-table on some occasions. Movable chairs and flat floors will make this possible.

Certainly the next few years promise to be exciting ones in Protestant liturgical architecture as more congregations have the courage to go beyond the security of divided chancel or concert stage arrangements. If they probe deeply into the meaning of their worship they are likely to be successful in their experimentation. Then architecture can truly help the Church to realize itself as the body of Christ.

VII
That Which Is Seen

In the previous chapters we have considered church architecture from the standpoint of its function in common worship, that is, as liturgical architecture. Our concern has been with how the buildings work in providing the setting for common worship in the belief that this is the most important area of concern. Unless the liturgical factors are given first priority it is impossible to erect an adequate church building.

The basic problems of church architecture vary from age to age. The early Church was conscious of little other than the essentials of worship and thus it could safely proceed to elaboration in worship and architecture when persecution ceased. The Reformation called for a return to the fundamentals of worship, too much elaboration having obscured them. Our age is similar. We live in a time when the prime need in worship and church architecture is purification, a return to essentials. Others can elaborate on what we now do; our task is to seek the inner kernel of worship and to provide the most direct architectural setting for it. In many other types of architecture (such as school design) the stage of purification has already occurred and elaboration is under way. But church architecture in this country has scarcely reflected a real understanding of what the Church does in common worship and it is hard to see how it can progress till more congregations wrestle with these essentials.

It is only after the liturgical factors have been carefully worked out that we are justified in turning to a consideration of how the building looks. The mistakes of many new churches could have been avoided if building committees had concerned themselves first with how the building works and then with how it looks. Churches are not built primarily to create works of art, but to provide the setting for common worship. The appearance of the building is largely the responsibility of the architect; how it functions is the concern of the congregation. Frequently, however, projects in which great care has been taken in defining function enable the architect to produce buildings which are also esthetically outstanding.

For this reason we have left till last a consideration of how churches look. Only after the liturgical requirements have been thrashed out can the esthetic concerns be seen in due perspective. These will be discussed in brief form under three topics: a general approach to the emotive factors, the special problems of liturgical art, and the question of architectural style.

I

Despite the primacy of common worship there is no denying that Protestant churches are used to a certain degree for personal devotions. Indeed, liturgical worship is quite insufficient if it is not accompanied by the discipline of personal devotions. The two types of worship complement each other. Just as particular hours are set aside for common worship, so too personal devotions deserve special times. Let us look at these occasions of personal devotions.

Many Christians use the time before and after services of common worship for personal devotions. For some this is the only time during the week allotted to devotions. In most churches

organ music is provided during these periods. Increasingly congregations are being directed to the use of preparatory prayers
(often found in hymnals) or the reading of portions of the Bible
during these periods. Although many people still use this time as
a social occasion, the general tendency seems to be that of providing encouragement for them to use these periods for prayer,
meditation, and scripture reading.

It would be impossible to deny that personal devotions occur
during common worship and that some services encourage this
with moments of silent meditation and anthems. Such a practice
is questionable since it serves to interrupt the oneness engendered
by the common worship. Nevertheless, in performing our work
of common worship the feelings do remain, for to expect emotions to be completely absent at any time is to expect the worshiper to be less than fully human. Consequently the worshiper
will be aware of the emotive factors even in a liturgical service
though they will not then be his primary concern.

Most churches have some special services in which the primary
focus is on personal devotions, although they may be performed
in a group. For some unknown reason, these services usually occur in the afternoon or evening. Sacred concerts are held in many
churches today and the custom, particularly in Lutheran
churches, is a very old one. Every indication is that sacred concerts will continue to be held at Christmas and Easter and, in
larger churches, at other occasions throughout the year. In most
cases they are conducted solely by the choir and other musicians
and the congregation is allowed to use this opportunity for personal devotions, having little actual work to perform. Other
services which focus upon personal devotions include various
forms of prayer meetings, witness meetings, and altar prayers. In
some of these the personal devotions of individuals are shared
with the group but frequently only a few are involved and no
effort to make this common worship is considered necessary.

Churches are also used for personal devotions when no service is in progress. This is especially true of downtown churches which often remain open during the week or provide a meditation chapel for such purposes. It seems rather unlikely that Protestants will drive to a suburban church during the week to use the chapel for personal devotions, though small chapels in office buildings and places where people work might fulfill this purpose, as wayside shrines in Catholic lands have done for centuries.

These occasions of churches' being used for personal devotions have been cited simply to show that this is a significant function of church buildings albeit considerably less important than their liturgical function. The emotive factors, those factors which produce feelings that aid personal devotions, are certainly worthy of full attention once the requirements of common worship have been fully considered.

No clear and consistent plan of securing the proper emotive factors has been produced nor is any likely. Unlike the liturgical factors, the emotive factors are highly subjective and vary from individual to individual and from congregation to congregation. At best, all that can be said about them are certain general statements which admittedly are of limited usefulness.

Ironically, the emotive factors have often been at their best in a number of contemporary churches where most of the attention of those responsible for directing the architect was devoted to the liturgical factors. Some of these buildings are so characterized by a forthrightness of intention, a concentration on essentials, and an elimination of unessentials that their starkness in itself is far more emotive than any painted prettiness could have been. The churches of Rudolf Schwarz in Germany give convincing proof of this.

Although most congregations cannot engage a man of Schwarz's stature as architect, they would do well to consider the importance of choosing an architect carefully. This usually means visiting a number of his previous churches and other buildings rather than relying solely on photographs which can be

THAT WHICH IS SEEN

deceptive. Interviews with former clients can sometimes be helpful. Lastly, interviews with the architect are necessary. By and large, one will have to rely on the architect's skill in securing adequate emotive factors. The real responsibility of the congregation is to supply as explicit a program as is possible for the direction of the architect in the liturgical factors. In other words, the building committee must be prepared to tell the architect how the projected building is to work. The architect has the responsibility of determining how it will look although he would be unwise to do this without consulting the wishes of the congregation. The congregation does not possess the technical skill necessary to design the building. At one time churches were designed and erected by a local builder who often referred to books of plans. Today architecture is immensely more complicated so that even the architect may need to rely upon acoustical, lighting, and structural engineers.

If the congregation can present the architect with a clear formulation of the necessary liturgical factors, a good architect can usually be relied upon to achieve adequate emotive factors as well. His technical and artistic abilities help accomplish this but he cannot be expected to provide the theological information necessary for the liturgical factors. Thus a congregation should be concerned about how the building works and entrust how it looks, the emotive factors, to a competent architect. Give him the words and let him draw the lines.

The tools which modern science has supplied for the architect are many and varied but also exceedingly complex. Churches can be built now (such as St. Clement's, Alexandria, Va.) where daylight is excluded altogether and all lighting is carefully aimed at liturgical centers and spaces. Others (such as St. John's Lutheran, Midland, Mich.) rejoice in daylight pouring down upon the altar-table.

Equally important are the possibilities in color available now. There was a time, not so long ago, when dark wood paneling was somehow associated with piety and even so sophisticated an architect as Ralph Adams Cram filled his churches with dark wood. The possible colors and color combinations make their selection no task for an amateur since even slight differences in shade can give quite unexpected emotive results. Stained glass is used increasingly in abstract patterns to give colored light. Perhaps nothing is as beautiful as the warm splash of primary colors on gray stone. Some beautiful three dimensional effects are possible today with thick chipped glass set in a concrete or plastic matrix. This is lively even in windows facing north.

Proportions and shapes are much more flexible now than ever before. It is likely that we will see more free form churches such as Corbusier's Chapel at Ronchamp, Niemeyer's churches in Brasilia, or Pratt and Box's Church in Mesquite, Tex. The possibilities of textures are increasingly exciting with new wood products, greater use of raw concrete, plus a variety of other artificial products. All of these have tremendous emotive powers and depend upon the skill of the architect.

More and more churches are using such art forms as painting and sculpture in a decorative fashion. This should be distinguished from liturgical art, as such, which will be discussed later. Art which does not refer to the Object of our worship may be used for emotive effects in scenes from nature, figures, or abstractions. There should be a careful planning relationship between the artists and the architect since art has often destroyed the intentions of the architect. Our purpose is not to create a museum of religious art. Many churches have a memorials committee which is in charge of accepting and also rejecting proffered gifts of furnishings or works of art. Usually this committee should work in close conjunction with the architect so that the art becomes a part of the whole building, not a conflicting appendage.

Though not something visible, the question of music deserves some treatment under the heading of emotive factors, especially since, for better or worse, it is widely understood in this fashion. As we have seen, the singing of hymns is really a liturgical act in which the entire congregation performs an act of praise, thanksgiving, or affirmation as the case may be. But music also has an impressive role in Protestant worship as an emotive factor. This is true both of organ music and of choral music. Solos and quartets still occur too but apparently they are increasingly being replaced by full choirs.

The organ has become almost a standard appurtenance of large churches today though as late as the eighteenth century Congregationalists decried its presence. The organ has several functions in Protestant worship. It provides music before and after the service for personal devotions. During the service it has often been used for background music, sometimes excessively. It also provides a major help in the singing of hymns, doxologies, and other congregational responses. Thus its use is both emotive and liturgical.

The advice of a competent musician should be secured in planning for an organ. The type of organ in favor a few years ago is increasingly being replaced by organs built to specifications more suitable for playing baroque music. It should be more widely known that genuine pipe organs can frequently be secured for prices not greatly in excess of the electronic organ imitations which are widely marketed. The pipe organ can be built with the specific requirements of an individual congregation in mind and additional ranks of pipes can be added from time to time. The type of instrument desired should be considered during the planning process since the tone of an organ is very definitely affected by where the pipes are placed. The effectiveness of many a fine instrument has been destroyed by placing it in an unfortunate position or by surrounding it with textures unsuitable for the sound.

The role of the choir in Protestant worship is a highly perplexing problem. As we have seen, the choir became popular in parish churches throughout great segments of English-speaking Protestantism as a result of revivalism or romanticism. Yet to this day there remains considerable confusion of exactly what the function of the choir is in Protestant worship and there is no single good rationale for the existence of the choir in Protestantism. It is considered here primarily as an emotive factor since this seems to be the approach usually taken in describing its function. Four common concepts about the choir's functions are worth examining.

In many Protestant congregations the choir is used to create a musical effect in much the same fashion as the lighting, color, and textures create visual effects. The primary concern often seems to be in creating a feeling or atmosphere of worship. Frequently the words are of little importance, either by being untranslated, theologically banal, or the result of careless diction. The net result, frequently, is that choral music becomes a background and the anthems provide an occasion for personal devotions or a cover for the silent actions of offering or procession to the altar-table. The concern often shows itself in a preoccupation with making music as beautiful as possible and in this it becomes an important emotive factor.

Such a practice is not without drawbacks. In reducing music to a background an injustice is done to music itself much as with that piped into supermarkets as a pleasant inducement to buying. More serious is the concern about beauty as being consciously sought. There is nothing specifically holy about beauty. The frequently-quoted Psalm text about worshiping "the Lord in the beauty of holiness" would be better translated "Worship the Lord in holy array." Beauty is certainly not the end of Christian worship. Neither is it necessarily the end of good music for it could well be argued that great art usually seeks much more than beauty alone. Some of the composers of the nineteenth century, now so popular in choir repertories, may have felt this way but contemporary music often deliberately avoids any conventional prettiness.

A better concept of the choir's function is that of leading congregational singing. According to this theory, the members of the choir have some musical training while most of the congregation does not. Those in the choir provide both volume and harmony thus making it easier for the congregation to participate in the singing of hymns and responses even when unfamiliar. In this sense the choir functions as a liturgical factor. Presumably the choir has rehearsed new music and approaches it without the timidity that usually accompanies the introduction of new hymns. Unfortunately the theory has often proved better than the practice. All too frequently choirs subvert this function and instead of leading congregational singing they replace it altogether. In many congregations more and more of the music is performed by choirs and less and less by the congregation. No doubt the quality of the music improves when it is turned over to specialists but beauty alone may be less important than full congregational participation.

It is sometimes argued that the members of the choir participate in the ministry of the Word just as others do through reading the lessons and preaching. In this sense the choir makes statements and proclamations in much the same way as is done in the reading and preaching of the Word. Quite frequently anthems consist of scriptural passages or paraphrases. Handel's *Messiah* is probably the best-known example of this practice. The same argument is sometimes used to justify solos as personal confessions of faith. This contention seems to have some validity but it can be challenged on the grounds that few choirs seem to stick to texts entirely worthy of the term proclamation, that when they do the words are often difficult to follow, and that music (except for chanting) often provides a highly subjective form of exegesis which occasionally perverts texts entirely. Some of these abuses might be rectified if effective standards for texts could be established such as that limiting anthems to "the words of Holy Scripture or of the Book of Common Prayer" in the Episcopal Church.[1]

A fourth interpretation of the function of a choir, and probably the best, is that it serves to make an offering to God. In this way its work is liturgical rather than emotive for it makes an offering of work performed to the best of their ability by choir members, often literally having involved a sacrifice of their time. Thus anthems are offered, not for the benefit of the congregation but as a sacrifice to God. In this sense the choir exercises a representative function. But there are dangers in this, especially when choral music replaces congregational singing. It can lead to a professionalism in which the worshipers become more and more passive. Indeed this has happened in many churches. It would be even better if the entire congregation could offer the liturgy themselves instead of delegating portions to those with musical talents. Even when the choir conceives of its work as an offering there is danger that the congregation may use these intervals as opportunities to lapse into daydreaming or personal devotions in a fashion not possible in parts of the service demanding more action.

These concepts of music have been raised simply to show that music, whether its primary function be considered emotive or liturgical, must be seriously considered in planning a church. Chances are that unconsciously it has assumed an emotive function in the minds of most people. Yet, as indicated, it is certainly capable of several liturgical functions. Which of these predominate will dictate the location of the choir and organ console.

In most churches the organist directs the choir and it goes without saying that the console must be visible to the choir. Even where there is a choir director the console and choir must be likewise close. Thus the location of the choir will largely direct the

[1] *Book of Common Prayer*, p. viii.

location of the console with the additional factor that the organist often needs to see the minister and ushers at various times
during the service.

Many locations for the choir have been tried and none of them
are wholly successful. Probably the most familiar are the divided
chancel arrangement, popularized by the Cambridge Movement
and the concert choir, a relic of revivalism. To a large degree the
chancel arrangement reflects the work of the choir as an offering
but it tends to make this too exclusively a prerogative of choir
and clergy by separating the congregation from the altar-table.
The concert arrangement emphasizes the emotive conditioning
and also the note of proclamation, but it is hardly esthetically
attractive no matter how gaudy the choir robes may be. It also
gives the singers an undue prominence, making them the central
feature of the church rather than the liturgical centers.

In recent years various substitute positions have been found. A
gallery at the rear has been tried but the singers feel dissociated
from the congregation. A transept to one side of the nave has a
somewhat similar function but with the advantage that the singers
are not so isolated nor are they divided as in a chancel. Some
effective experiments have placed the choir behind a screen behind or to one side of the altar-table. This has the advantage of
focusing on their work of offering rather than their appearance.
One of the best situations seems to be that of placing the choir
in a special portion of the nave, often toward the front with the
deliberate intention of helping them lead congregational singing.
This in some ways recovers the ancient basilican arrangement
but it does cause the problem of locating the console and the
problem of the choir director's being too prominent. Some choirs
have even scattered their members throughout the congregation
with the primary intention of stimulating congregational singing.

Certainly every indication is that we need more serious thought
about the function of the choir in Protestant worship. Obviously
it has a place in the sacred concert in larger churches but this is

not the normal Sunday service. What is the choir's function in common worship? Should it be limited to the occasional sacred concert? Most congregations have simply taken the choir for granted without raising these questions, yet they must be asked as a part of any serious building project.

As can be seen, the emotive requirements of a church are difficult to deal with because they are so subjective. Many of these factors have only limited accessibility to various members. Not only are some people tone deaf when it comes to music, but many may have little responsiveness to color, light, shapes, or textures. Thus the emotive factors cannot be determined with the precision of the liturgical factors. Many variables and imponderables will remain precisely because people react so differently to the same emotive factors.

II

Increasingly Protestant churches are making use of liturgical art. Definitions of liturgical art vary but for our present purpose it can be defined by its function. Liturgical art, then, is art that is used in common worship and usually represents some aspect or act of the Object of our worship. This distinguishes it not only from religious art in general but also from art used decoratively or for devotional purposes. Thus a painting of the Good Samaritan could be called religious art but it would hardly be used as liturgical art. Indeed it is rather difficult to draw any line between religious art and other art since the style of an artist, painting supposedly secular subjects, may reveal religious insight through the manner in which he paints. Much art is widely used in churches in a purely decorative fashion. As such it is one of the emotive factors discussed above.

Liturgical art, then, is determined primarily by its usage in common worship and secondly by its subject matter's being concerned with the divinity. Usually, but not always, it is associated with the liturgical centers. Thus a descending dove upon a baptismal font represents both the historical occasion of the baptism of Jesus and the contemporary reception or acknowledgement of the Spirit in baptism. An angel with a trumpet upon a pulpit (once a favorite Protestant symbol) proclaims the nativity of Our Lord but also represents the current proclamation of preaching. A painting of the head of Christ helps us recognize the presence of the Object of our worship.

One of the primary functions of liturgical art is to make us aware of the presence of the holy, making visible that which is invisible. This does not mean that liturgical art has any particular efficacy in making God present but it does help bring His presence directly to our consciousness. A photograph can bring to mind loved ones even though they are not actually present. We keep such pictures on our desks and in our wallets because they make us feel closer to those they represent. Something similar happens in liturgical art but here the case is altered since God is actually fully present in our worship though invisible. Liturgical art makes us conscious of what is already there. In this sense it has a very important function in common worship.

There has always been a fear in Judaism and Christianity lest liturgical art might be confused with the Object it represents. Historically several Protestant traditions have felt that they could not sanction the use of any liturgical art whatsoever. This is not because they denied the power of such art, indeed it is because they took it so seriously. But the second commandment forbade the worship of images and this could be interpreted as including any representation which might become idolatrous. This danger does not seem to be a present possibility and it is unlikely that people today would confuse a bit of liturgical art with the deity. Indeed the problem is the opposite, that liturgical art may not be treated with the full seriousness it deserves.

In liturgical art physical objects of the natural world are used to represent that which is supernatural. To a large extent this influences the style of liturgical art as well as the subject matter. Much of the art used in churches today fails as liturgical art because it is simply a naturalistic reproduction of the appearance of objects. Frequently it does little more than give a photographic image of something we already know. But good liturgical art goes beyond this in trying to convey the very being of what is presented. Its concern is not with appearances but with the reality behind the appearances. Much of the art used in churches today hardly penetrates the surface. Thus the very popular paintings of Jesus by such artists as Sallman, Hofmann, and Christy represent Jesus so naturalistically that it is hard to realize that their subject is God Incarnate rather than a benevolent big brother. Theologically they are inadequate because they only represent one dimension of God's activity in Christ, the most obvious one, the human form. Other painters such as Rouault seek to penetrate the surface and to depict the reality of the Godhead present in flesh. In these paintings and other ancient and modern works true liturgical art appears, for the physical object (painting, statue) leads us to ultimate reality.

Frequently the Church has resorted to the use of symbols to point to divine realities. These symbols provide a kind of sign language representing that which cannot be portrayed in visible form, or they serve as a shortcut in making statements, particularly about historical events. Thus the dove is a symbol of the Holy Spirit Who obviously cannot be depicted in a visible form. The phoenix is a symbol of the resurrection, which would be very difficult to portray.

The problem, however, is to make certain that these symbols are inherent in the liturgy. Symbols of water or the colors and forms associated with water are particularly appropriate around fonts and baptisteries for they show forth the actions performed in baptism. On the other hand, much symbolism used in churches may simply be used decoratively in the same fashion as wallpaper in a home. There are some real dangers in allowing symbolism to dictate the form or arrangement of a building. Churches have been designed in the shape of a crown of thorns, a fish, and a ship. The question which must be raised here is, "So what?" Do these symbols inhere in the liturgy or are they imposed upon it? If they express the liturgy they are fine but if they are merely symbolic whimsies they may do more harm than good.

Liturgical art has definite restrictions on its subject matter and style.[2] It must be communal in nature. Good liturgical art grows out of the life of worship of the Christian community. It is not noted for originality and invention in subject matter though the treatment may vary. Liturgical art is not the place for the artist to assert his individuality. Indeed liturgical art has a certain impersonality since it must be shared by all the worshiping community. This was supremely true in much medieval art where even the name of the artist was not considered worth preserving. He worked within a community which had explicit ideas about its worship and the Object of its worship. The artist worked within the bounds prescribed by the community's experience of divine reality. This is not to say that the artist must be a Christian. Some of the art in the ancient catacombs was possibly produced by non-Christian artists who were working in the service and under the guidance of the Christian community. In our own time the same thing has happened in the Church of Assy, France, where some of the great artists outside the Church contributed works of art under the careful direction of the clergy. Just as the architect must know the liturgical function of a church before he can design a successful building, so the artist must understand the life of the community before he can produce liturgical art for it.

It is only when liturgical art grows out of the life of the com-

---

[2] Cf. Cyril C. Richardson, "Some Reflections on Liturgical Art," *Union Seminary Quarterly Review,* VIII (1953), 24–8.

munity that it is accessible to all members of the congregation. Essentially it expresses the faith which makes the Church one. The place for personal subjective references is very greatly limited. Liturgical art is a very disciplined variety of art and it is not surprising that there has been relatively little good liturgical art in recent years as compared to a fairly large amount of religious art. Perhaps this is partly due to the fact that congregations have been reluctant to be explicit about the subject matter of liturgical art lest this be an imposition upon the artist's integrity. For art meant to be used for purely decorative purposes there is some object in protesting a too close regimentation of the artist. But liturgical art by its communal nature is different. It cannot reflect the faith which makes the community one unless the artist knows and respects this faith whether he accepts it or not. Non-Christian artists can create good liturgical art if they know the faith which they are serving.

This means that a theological effort is necessary in commissioning liturgical art just as in commissioning liturgical architecture. Unless the congregation can articulate its faith it can hardly expect to secure adequate liturgical art. There are dangers, to be sure, that congregations can be so excessively literal in their demands upon an artist that he is left with the choice of producing inferior art or none. But the more usual danger is that of theological fuzziness in which the artist is given free reign with no guidance. In liturgical art the artist is not finding self-expression but is expressing the faith of a community. This makes it quite different from other types of art.

Liturgical art, because of its communal nature, is strongly affected by the traditions of the Christian community. Thus no congregation comes to the problem *de novo*, though they may make some innovations. Just as the faith itself has been delivered to us from others, so we receive a tradition in liturgical art both in subjects represented naturally and symbols. These have been passed on for generations so that some of the symbols present in the catacombs are still found in churches today.[3] These signs and symbols link us to other Christians just as the words and acts we use in worship do.

Though there is definitely a tradition in liturgical art regarding subject matter, the contents are not completely unchanging. Historical research can trace the introduction of new subjects and symbols, as well as their passing from currency. It is just as important to remember that symbols die as that new ones arise. Thus the pomegranate and the peacock were favorite symbols of the resurrection at one time but would be almost meaningless to contemporaries. Symbols die and it is probably better not to try to revive them. One sees the strange phenomenon of many congregations, having built a new building and filled it with symbols, obliged to compile a booklet explaining the meaning of these symbols. So common a practice has this become that we fail to recognize what an extraordinary example it is of putting the cart before the horse. If the symbols grew out of the life of the congregation, explanation would be superfluous. Actually what has usually happened is that the symbols have been culled from some book on the subject or simply ordered from a church goods catalogue. Such symbols are esoteric and antiquarian in nature and have no relation to the life of the congregation. Far better to do without symbols than to use those which have no meaning!

On the other hand, to produce new symbols is no easy task. For the present we are probably largely limited to symbols of the life of Christ (particularly those commemorated in the Christian year), and those reflecting our acts of worship. Even these must come out of the life and experience of the congregation before

[3] Cf. Walter Lowrie, *Art in the Early Church* (New York: Pantheon, 1947); Charles R. Morey, *Early Christian Art; an Outline of the Evolution of Style and Iconography in Sculpture and Painting from Antiquity to the Eighth Century* (Princeton: Princeton University Press, 1942); D. Talbot Rice, *The Beginnings of Christian Art* (Nashville: Abingdon, 1957).

they have any legitimacy for those in the church. Symbols do not have life vicariously. They either have it because those who use them participate in the realities they represent or they have none. In the early days of our Republic symbols of liberty, eagles, and pictures of Washington were widely used. They reflected the national experience of freedom and had a spontaneous and ecstatic character. This is the only type of symbol which is genuine. Some of the old symbols (such as the cross) certainly convey this reality but many (such as the pomegranate) do not.

One other factor is operative in liturgical art. This is its religious power, its ability to convey a sense of the divine. This numinous quality makes liturgical art different from much other art. It was this quality which made Protestants in the sixteenth century destroy so much liturgical art. It was not that they felt such art was impotent but precisely because they recognized that it made the divine so present that in ignorance people might confuse liturgical art with that which it represented. They destroyed liturgical art to safeguard the transcendence of God over His creation.

Only when art turned to a more completely naturalistic rendering of the appearance of things could it be safely tolerated. But then it had no religious power. It could be safely hung in art galleries. Crucifixes, nudes, and landscapes hung in the same galleries, treated alike as compositions rather than means of conveying the divine presence. The art of the nineteenth century produced very little good liturgical art since most of the concern was with reproducing the visible world.

In our own time artists have turned again to painting the unseen world with its awe and mystery. Such art seeks to penetrate the essence of things and to show more than the surface. It has the dimension of depth. Here there is the possibility of genuine liturgical art. Whether the church will give the necessary guidance to artists and commission them to produce liturgical art or not remains to be seen.

The current indications show that Protestantism is moving to a greater readiness to use liturgical art in its liturgical centers and the spaces which surround them. This is not an easy decision. Though the possibility of confusing the divine with the object representing it seems a bit unlikely to sophisticated man today, Protestants do well to realize the danger of making the divine too apparently accessible. The historical protest against a localized divinity is not without very good theological substance.

On the other hand there is an opposite form of idolatry to which Protestants have not been equally sensitive. This is the possibility that worship be perverted into an egocentric satisfying of our own emotions. In its most unguarded forms, worship cultivated as a means of satisfying our feelings can be a pernicious form of idolatry for it is essentially service of self. Liturgical art can be a means of preventing this type of idolatry by calling to our attention that the object of our worship is other than ourselves. It can then be an important factor in preventing the idolatry of egocentric worship. In this way it can make a vital contribution to Protestant worship.

III

We have left till last the question of architectural style though this is where most discussions begin. This has been done deliberately with the belief that style is not the first question to be decided. Indeed, if the liturgical questions are discussed carefully it is possible that contemporary architecture will appear as the only real possibility especially when a novel floor plan seems necessary. This will not always be so obvious in some instances. Of course, in some parts of the country it is almost taken for granted now that contemporary architectural forms will be used. In more conservative areas style still remains a live question though everywhere contemporary forms are becoming more and more common in churches.

As we have tried to show, the most important consideration for the congregation to consider in a church building is how it functions in common worship. This means that function is the primary concern and that appearance comes after this. Ironically, the plans of many so-called contemporary churches have been based more upon appearance than upon function. Yet one of the keynotes of contemporary architecture in America has been the dictum, "Form follows function." This means that the purposes for which a building is designed should determine its appearance, even though visual delight may be one function in many buildings. Thus utility is a foremost consideration. Unfortunately what is now called contemporary architecture is often a hackneyed assortment of clichés, such as flat roofs, large glass areas, and sparse ornamentation. The regularity with which some of the better known examples of contemporary church architecture are copied, imitated, and watered-down regardless of a congregation's traditions and needs shows that contemporary and functional are far from being synonymous.

An astoundingly large number of the "contemporary" churches built in the last decade have been contemporary only in appearance. In many cases their liturgical arrangement may have been derived from that suited for a congregation of medieval peasants. Yet the same arrangement has been imposed upon Baptists, Methodists, and Presbyterians in countless American suburbs and we have called it contemporary because the details of the building were of our time. Yet when it comes to providing the setting for our worship these buildings are romantic, not functional. Many people would hardly accept such unfunctional designs in houses (though they might in their automobiles!). It is indeed surprising how unfunctional many of our churches are.

If one were to have his choice of a building which reproduced many of the details and materials of a building built in one of the traditional styles but which was so planned that its liturgical centers and spaces were a direct outgrowth of the congregation's worship, or a contemporary style building which repeated an outmoded liturgical arrangement, the choice might well go to the former building. In a real sense it would be more functional than one which simply imitated an obsolete arrangement no matter how up-to-date its materials and details might be.

Fortunately this choice is not necessary. In most cases the process we have outlined in Chapter II of determining liturgical arrangement by analysis of function will probably also suggest the same approach to the question of style. It will be seen that contemporary architecture is infinitely adaptable to new shapes and forms. A gothic dome is a contradiction in terms; a hexagonal Georgian building will lead to basic problems particularly if a portico, or two, or three are desired. But contemporary architecture is not inhibited by the peculiarities of any shape. Thus it can give considerably greater freedom for experimentation in liturgical architecture. Free-form architecture can utilize shapes never before created if the liturgical requirements indicate such needs. A free-form building in classic style would be an absurdity; in contemporary materials and design it is readily possible. Thus the greatest argument for contemporary architecture in church building is that it can encompass so many shapes that would have to be rejected if other styles were to be chosen. With contemporary architecture one can do almost anything necessary. This is not true of period architecture.

There is another important argument for contemporary architecture in church building though it is not a liturgical one. This is the image the church makes in the minds of those who do not enter its doors. Church members are not the only ones affected by church architecture. Many people have their concept of the Church largely determined by the exterior of the churches they know. One army chaplain found that he could start a discussion of Christianity with any group of soldiers simply by referring to the way church buildings looked. Everyone had seen churches whether they were churchmen or not. From this experience they

had formed some concepts, accurate or not, of the purposes for
which the Church existed.

Business firms are highly conscious of the importance of architecture in creating a public image. Insurance firms are likely to
erect substantial solid structures. Other businesses vie with each
other to erect edifices which suggest progressive forward-look-
ing institutions. In each case the building is an asset or a liability
in its testimony to the firm's character.

The same thing is true of churches. Most people who pass a
church's door never enter it. But they do form impressions of the
Church from the physical church. There are questions which
consciously or unconsciously arise in people's minds: "Is this
building and its purposes relevant for me? Or of no particular interest?" People are inclined to wonder if the institution the
building represents has anything to say to them really worth
hearing. If the church building suggests retreat from the modern
world it is apt to indicate a failure to take the Incarnation of God
in man's form seriously. Christ came into a world of flux and
change rather than into a timeless void. "Is the Church's message
significant?" Not all buildings encourage further inquiry by
suggesting that the Church has anything significant to say. Too
often these buildings are but pale copies of obsolete styles and
insignificant obscurities. Finally, men ask, "Is it sincere?" And
here many buildings, both traditional and contemporary, bear a
bad witness for they have concerned themselves with appearances and façades. No one is deceived by the false storefronts of
frontier towns but many churches have also built pretentious
façades with little relationship to what is behind them. In this
sense the question of style is important for it is a means of proclamation. The honesty and forthrightness of a building designed
from the inside out for its liturgical functions is often apparent on
the outside and makes the building an important witness to those
outside the Church. Likewise contemporary style in a building
truly functional can be a means of proclaiming the Gospel. A

building which does not give a positive witness betrays the faith.

For those who do enter the church, the interior is a means of teaching what it is to be the Church and what the Church does. Whereas the exterior can only proclaim in a general way the relevance, significance, and sincerity of the Church to men's lives, the interior in a very explicit manner shows forth what it is the Church does in its life together: study, social fellowship, and above all else worship. It is especially important that the building affirms that it represents a community for whom worship is the primary act that constitutes and expresses the oneness of the group.

Architecture, then, can be a means of teaching those who enter the Church what it is to be one in Christ. Liturgical architecture provides the space and tools in which the central acts of the Christian life are performed in the common worship of God. The building is indeed a most important concern of the Church since it provides all the physical conditions necessary for a crucial part of our work done in God's service, our common worship.

Select Bibliography

I. HISTORICAL PERIODS

General Histories:
Comper, J. Ninian. *Of the Christian Altar and the Buildings Which Contain It.* London: S.P.C.K., 1950.
Conant, Kenneth J. "The Expression of Religion in Architecture" in *The Arts and Religion.* Edited by Albert Edward Bailey. New York: Macmillan Co., 1944.
Cope, Gilbert. *Symbolism in the Bible and the Church.* London: S.C.M. Press, 1959.
Davies, J. G. *The Architectural Setting of Baptism.* London: Barrie and Rockliff, 1962.
Ferguson, George. *Signs & Symbols in Christian Art.* New York: Oxford University Press, 1961.
Minchin, Basil. *Outward and Visible.* London: Darton, Longman & Todd, 1961.
Short, Ernest. *A History of Religious Architecture.* 3rd edition; New York: W. W. Norton & Co., n.d.

Early Christian and Byzantine:
Davies, J. G. *The Origin and Development of Early Christian Church Architecture.* New York: Philosophical Library, 1953.
Hoddinott, R. F. *Early Byzantine Churches in Macedonia and Southern Serbia: A Study of the Origins and Initial Development of East Christian Art.* London: Macmillan, 1963.

Lowrie, Walter. *Art in the Early Church.* New York: Pantheon Books, 1947.

Simson, Otto von. *Sacred Fortress: Byzantine Art and Statecraft in Ravenna.* Chicago: University of Chicago Press, 1948.

Strzygowski, Josef. *Origin of Christian Church Art: New Facts and Principles of Research.* Translated by O. M. Dalton and H. J. Braunholtz. Oxford: Clarendon Press, 1923.

Van der Meer, F. and Christine Mohrmann. *Atlas of the Early Christian World.* Translated and edited by Mary F. Hedlund and H. H. Rowley. London: Nelson, 1958.

Wheler, Sir George. *An Account of the Churches or Places of Assembly of the Primitive Christians; from the Churches of Tyre, Jerusalem, and Constantinople: Described by Eusebius and Ocular Observations of Several Very Ancient Edifices of Churches yet Extant in those Parts; With a Seasonable Application.* London: R. Clavell, 1689.

Medieval:

Aubert, Marcel and Simone Goubet. *Gothic Cathedrals in France and Their Treasures.* Translated by Lionel and Miriam Kochan and George Millard. London: Nicholas Kaye Ltd., 1959.

Conant, Kenneth J. *Carolingian and Romanesque Architecture, 800–1200.* (The Pelican History of Art.) Harmondsworth, Middlesex: Penguin Books, 1959.

Frankl, Paul. *The Gothic: Literary Sources and Interpretations through Eight Centuries.* Princeton: Princeton University Press, 1960.

Gall, Ernst. *Cathedrals and Abbey Churches of the Rhine.* Translated and adapted by Olive Cook. New York: Harry N. Abrams, Inc., 1963.

Harvey, John. *The Cathedrals of Spain.* London: B. T. Batsford Ltd., 1957.

Mâle, Emile. *The Gothic Image: Religious Art in France of the Thirteenth Century.* Translated by Dora Nussey. New York: Harper & Bros., 1958.

Panofsky, Erwin. *Gothic Architecture and Scholasticism.* New York: Meridian Books, 1957.

Simson, Otto von. *The Gothic Cathedral: Origins of Gothic Architecture and the Medieval Concept of Order: With an Appendix on the Proportions of the South Tower of Chartres Cathedral.* New York: Pantheon, 1956.

Post-Reformation:
American Church Silver of the Seventeenth and Eighteenth Centuries with a Few Pieces of Domestic Plate. Boston: Museum of Fine Arts, 1911.

Betjeman, John. "Nonconformist Architecture," *Architectural Review,* LXXXVIII (1940), 161–74.

Bourke, John. *Baroque Churches of Central Europe.* Revised edition; London: Faber and Faber, 1963.

Briggs, Martin S. *Puritan Architecture and Its Future.* London: Lutterworth, 1946.

Broderick, Robert C. *Historic Churches of the United States.* New York: Wilfred Funk, Inc., 1958.

Cram, Ralph Adams. *American Church Building of Today.* New York: Architectural Book Publishing Co., Inc., 1929.

DeZurko, Edward R. *Early Kansas Churches.* Manhattan, Kansas: The College, 1949.

Drummond, Andrew L. *The Church Architecture of Protestantism: An Historical and Constructive Study.* Edinburgh: T. & T. Clark, 1934.

Embury, Aymar, II. *Early American Churches.* Garden City: Doubleday, Page & Co., 1914.

Faris, John T. *Old Churches and Meeting Houses in and around Philadelphia.* Philadelphia: J. B. Lippincott Co., 1926.

Garvan, Anthony. "The Protestant Plain Style before 1630," *Journal of the Society of Architectural Historians,* IX (1950), 5–13.

Haskin, Frederic J. *Historic Churches in the United States.* Washington: c. 1938.

Holisher, Desider. *The House of God.* New York: Crown Publishers, 1946.

Jones, Ronald P. *Nonconformist Church Architecture.* London: Lindsey Press, 1914.

Morrison, Hugh. *Early American Architecture from the First Colonial Settlements to the National Period.* New York: Oxford University Press, 1952.

Ridgely, Helen West. *The Old Brick Churches of Maryland.* New York: Anson D. F. Randolph and Co., 1894.

Rines, Edward F. *Old Historic Churches of America: Their Romantic History and Their Traditions.* New York: Macmillan Co., 1936.

Rose, Harold W. *The Colonial Houses of Worship in America: Built in the English Colonies before the Republic, 1607–1789, and Still Standing.* New York: Hastings House, 1963.

Rosenau, Helen. "The Synagogue and Protestant Church Architecture," *Journal of the Warburg and Courtauld Institutes,* IV (1940–41), 80–84.

Trimen, Andrew. *Church and Chapel Architecture, from the Earliest Period to the Present Time, with an Account of the Hebrew Church; to Which are Added One Thousand Authenticated Mouldings, Selected from the Best Examples Which This Country Contains.* London: Longmans, Brown, Green, and Longmans, 1848.

Upjohn, Hobart B. *Churches in Eight American Colonies Differing in Elements of Design.* New York: R. F. Whitehead, c. 1929.

Vereinigung Berliner Architekten. *Der Kirchenbau des Protestantismus von der Reformation bis zur Gegenwart.* Berlin: Kommissions-Verlag von Ernst Toeche, 1893.

Wallace, Philip B. and William Allen Dunn. *Colonial Churches and Meeting Houses in Pennsylvania, New Jersey, and Delaware.* New York: Architectural Book Publishing Co., Inc., 1931.

Wallington, Nellie Urner. *Historic Churches of America.* New York: Duffield & Co., 1907.

Contemporary:

Atkinson, C. Harry. *Building and Equipping for Christian Education.* New York: National Council of Churches of Christ in the U.S.A., 1956.

Biedrzynski, Richard. *Kirchen Unserer Zeit.* Munich: Hirmer Verlag, 1958.

Christ-Janer, Albert and Mary Mix Foley. *Modern Church Architecture: A Guide to the Form and Spirit of 20th Century Religious Buildings.* New York: McGraw-Hill Book Co., 1962.

Clark, William S. *Building the New Church.* Jenkintown: Religious Publishing Co., 1957.

Conover, E. M. (ed.). *Planning Church Buildings.* New York: National Council of the Churches of Christ in the U.S.A., 1945.

Fiddes, Victor. *The Architectural Requirements of Protestant Worship.* Toronto: Ryerson Press, 1961.

Frey, Edward S. *This Before Architecture.* Jenkintown, Pennsylvania: Foundation Books, 1963.

Hammond, Peter. *Liturgy and Architecture.* London: Barrie and Rockliff, 1960.

—— (ed.). *Towards a Church Architecture.* London: Architectural Press, 1962.

Hess, Robert. *Moderne Kirchliche Kunst in der Schweiz.* Zürich: NZN Buchverlag, 1951.

Hoefler, Richard C. *Designed for Worship: A Study of the Furniture, Vessels, Linens, Paraments, and Vestments of Worship.* Columbia, S. C.: State Printing Co., 1963.

Kellenbach, Hans, D. Heinrich Laag, and P. Poscharsky (eds.) *Die Problematik des Modernen Kirchenbaues.* Marburg/Lahn and Arnoldshain: 1960.

Leach, William H. *Protestant Church Building: Planning, Financing, Designing.* New York: Abingdon-Cokesbury, 1948.

Lockett, William (ed.). *The Modern Architectural Setting of the Liturgy.* London: S.P.C.K., 1964.

McClinton, Katharine Morrison. *The Changing Church: Its Architecture, Art, and Decoration.* New York: Morehouse-Gorham, 1957.

Mills, Edward D. *The Modern Church.* London: Architectural Press, 1956.

Pfammatter, Ferdinand. *Betonkirchen.* Einsiedeln/Zürich/Köln: Benziger Verlag, 1948.

Pichard, Joseph. *Modern Church Architecture.* Translated by Ellen Callmann. New York: Orion Press, 1962.

Ramelli, A. Cassi. *Edifici Per Il Culto: Chiese Cattoliche Protestanti e Ortodosse; Moschee, Singoghe; Costruzioni Monastiche e Cimiteriali.* 3rd edition; Milan: Antonio Vallardi, 1953.

Regamey, P. R. *Art Sacré aus XX⁰ Siècle.* Paris: Editions du Cerf, 1952.

Roulin, Eugène Augustin. *Modern Church Architecture.* Translated by C. Cornelis Cragie and John A. Southwell. St. Louis: B. Herder Book Co., 1947.

Scotford, John R. *When You Build Your Church.* Great Neck: Doniger & Raughley Inc., 1955.

Shear, John Knox. (ed.). *Religious Buildings for Today*. New York: F. W. Dodge Corp., 1957.

Sixty Post-War Churches. London: Incorporated Church Building Society, 1956.

Thiry, Paul, Richard M. Bennett, and Henry L. Kamphoefner. *Churches & Temples*. New York: Reinhold Publishing Corp., 1953.

Watkin, William Ward. *Planning and Building the Modern Church*. New York: F. W. Dodge Corp., 1951.

Weyres, Willy. *Neue Kirchen im Erzbistum Köln*. Düsseldorf: Schwann Verlag, 1957.

Weyres, Willy, Otto Bartning, et al. *Kirchen: Handbuch für den Kirchenbau*. Munich: Verlag Georg D. W. Callwey, 1959.

White, James F. "Church Architecture: Some Standards," *Christian Century*, LXXVI (1959), 196–7.

—— "Some Contemporary Experiments in Liturgical Architecture," *Religion in Life*, XXX (1961), 285–95.

II. SPECIFIC TRADITIONS

Roman Catholic:

Anson, Peter F. *Churches, Their Plan and Furnishings*. Milwaukee: Bruce, 1948.

Baer, Kurt and Hugo Rudinger. *Architecture of the California Missions*. Berkeley and Los Angeles: University of California Press, 1958.

Brooks, Charles M., Jr., *Texas Missions; Their Romance and Architecture*. Dallas: Dealey and Lowe, 1936.

Collins, Monsignor. *The Church Edifice and Its Appointments*. Westminster, Md.: Newman Press, 1946.

Documents for Sacred Architecture. Collegeville, Minnesota: Liturgical Press, 1957.

Henze, Anton and Theodor Filthaut. *Contemporary Church Art*. Translated by Cecily Hastings and edited by Maurice Lavanoux. New York: Sheed & Ward, 1956.

Kubler, George. *The Religious Architecture of New Mexico in the Colonial Period and Since the American Occupation*. Colorado Springs: Taylor Museum, 1940.

O'Connell, J. *Church Building and Furnishing: The Church's Way; A Study in Liturgical Law*. London: Burns & Oates, 1955.

O'Donnell, Patrick (ed.). *Churches for Tomorrow.* Cincinnati: F. & W. Publishing Co., n.d.

Reinhold, H. A. *Speaking of Liturgical Architecture.* Notre Dame: Liturgical Programs, University of Notre Dame, 1952.

Schwarz, Rudolf. *The Church Incarnate: The Sacred Function of Christian Architecture.* Translated by Cynthia Harris. Chicago: Henry Regnery Co., 1958.

Seasoltz, Kevin R. *The House of God.* New York: Herder and Herder, 1963.

Church of England:

Addleshaw, G. W. O. and Frederick Etchells. *The Architectural Setting of Anglican Worship: An Inquiry into the Arrangements for Public Worship in the Church of England from the Reformation to the Present Day.* London: Faber & Faber, 1948.

Anson, Peter F. *Fashions in Church Furnishings, 1840–1940.* London: Faith Press, 1960.

Clarke, Basil F. L. *Anglican Cathedrals Outside the British Isles.* London: S. P. C. K., 1958.

—— *The Building of the Eighteenth-Century Church.* London: S.P.C.K., 1963.

—— *Church Builders of the Nineteenth Century: A Study of the Gothic Revival in England.* London: S. P. C. K., 1938.

Cobb, Gerald. *The Old Churches of London.* 3rd edition; London: B. T. Batsford, 1948.

Cope, Gilbert (ed.). *Making the Building Serve the Liturgy; Studies in the Re-ordering of Churches.* London: A. R. Mowbray & Co., 1962.

The Ecclesiologist, vols. I–XXIX. Cambridge: 1841–45; London: 1846–68.

Fürst, Viktor. *The Architecture of Sir Christopher Wren.* London: Lund Humphries, 1956.

Minchin, Basil. *The Celebration of the Eucharist Facing the People.* Bristol: Published by the author, n. d.

Whiffen, Marcus. *Stuart and Georgian Churches: The Architecture of the Church of England outside London; 1603–1837.* London: B. T. Batsford, 1948.

White, James F. *The Cambridge Movement: The Ecclesiologists and the Gothic Revival.* Cambridge: Cambridge University Press, 1962.

Young, Elizabeth and Wayland Young. *Old London Churches*. London: Faber & Faber Ltd., 1956.

Protestant Episcopal:
Betts, Darby Wood (ed.). *Architecture and the Church*. Greenwich: Seabury Press, 1952.
Brock, Henry Irving. *Colonial Churches in Virginia*. Richmond: Dale Press, 1930.
Colonial Churches in the Original Colony of Virginia. 2nd edition; Richmond: Southern Churchman Co., 1908.
Dorsey, Stephen P. *Early English Churches in America, 1607–1807*. New York: Oxford University Press, 1952.
Mason, George Carrington. *Colonial Churches of Tidewater Virginia*. Richmond: Whittet and Shepperson, 1945.
Rawlings, James S. *Virginia's Colonial Churches: An Architectural Guide*. Richmond: Garrett & Massie, 1963.
Shepherd, Massey H., Jr. et al. (eds.). *Before the Holy Table: A Guide to the Celebration of the Holy Eucharist, Facing the People, According to the Book of Common Prayer*. Greenwich: Seabury Press, 1956.
Sherman, Jonathan G. (ed.). *Church Buildings and Furnishings: A Survey of Requirements*. Greenwich: Seabury Press, 1958.
White, James F. "Theology and Architecture in America: A Study of Three Leaders," in *A Miscellany of American Christianity; Essays in Honor of H. Shelton Smith*. Edited by Stuart C. Henry. Durham, N. C.: Duke University Press, 1963.
Wigmore, Francis Marion. *The Old Parish Churches of Virginia*. Washington: U. S. Government Printing Office, 1929.

Presbyterian and Reformed:
Ark: 10 Jaar Kerkbouw, special issue of *Forum*, XII (1957).
Bakhuizen van den Brink, J. N. (ed. and contributor). *Protestantsche Kerkbouw. Een Bundel Studies*. Arnhem: S. Gouda Quint–D. Brouwer en Zoon, 1946.
Fifer, Duane Virgil. "Christian Art in the Place and Form of Presbyterian Worship; a Historical Survey of Church Architecture and Ecclesiastical Art from the Standpoint of the Presbyterian Church." Unpublished Th. M. thesis, Princeton Theological Seminary, 1956.

Hageman, Howard G. "Liturgical Place," *Princeton Seminary Bulletin*, LVI (1963), 29–39.

Hay, George. *The Architecture of Scottish Post-Reformation Churches, 1560–1843*. Oxford: Clarendon Press, 1957.

Hervormde Kerkbouw na 1945. The Hague: Uitgave van Boekencentrum, 1957.

Julien, Carl and Daniel W. Hollis. *Look to the Rock: One Hundred Ante-bellum Presbyterian Churches of the South*. Richmond: John Knox Press, 1961.

Lindsay, Ian G. *The Scottish Parish Kirk*. Edinburgh: Saint Andrew Press, 1960.

Massa, Conrad H. "Architectural Implications in Recent Trends in Reformed Liturgy," *Princeton Seminary Bulletin*, LIV (1961), 48–56.

Nederlands Nieuwe Kerken. Amsterdam: Uitgeverij G. van Saane, 1948.

Nichols, James H. and Leonard J. Trinterud. *The Architectural Setting for Reformed Worship*. Revised edition; Chicago: Presbytery of Chicago, 1960.

Ozinga, M. D. *De Protestantsche Kerkenbouw in Nederland van Hervorming tot Franschen Tijd*. Amsterdam: H. J. Paris, 1929.

Robinson, William Childs. *Architecture Appropriate for Reformed Worship*. Weaverville, North Carolina: Southern Presbyterian Journal, [1960].

Congregational:

Austin, Richard C. "The Meetinghouse of Colonial New England as an Expression of Puritan Theology." Unpublished B. D. thesis, Union Theological Seminary, 1959.

Bacon, Dolores. *Old New England Churches and Their Children*. New York: Doubleday Page & Co., 1906.

Bellows, Robert P. *An Architectural Monograph: Country Meeting Houses along the Massachusetts-New Hampshire Line*. New York: R. F. Whitehead, c. 1925.

Crawford, Mary C. *The Romance of Old New England Churches*. Boston: L. C. Page & Co., 1903.

Donnelly, Marian Card. "New England Meetinghouses in the Seventeenth Century," *Old-Time New England*, XLVII (1957), 85–99.

Garvan, Anthony N. B. *Architecture and Town Planning in Colonial Connecticut*. New Haven: Yale University Press, 1951.

Kelly, J. Frederick. *Early Connecticut Meetinghouses: Being an Account of the Church Edifices Built before 1830 Based Chiefly upon Town and Parish Records.* 2 vols. New York: Columbia University Press, 1948.

Lathrop, Elsie. *Old New England Churches.* Rutland, Vermont: Tuttle Publishing Co. Inc., 1938.

Maine Writers Research Club. *Historic Churches and Homes of Maine, with Photographic Illustrations.* Portland, Me.: Falmouth Book House, 1937.

Marlowe, George Francis. *Churches of Old New England: Their Architecture and Their Architects, Their Pastors and Their People.* New York: Macmillan, 1947.

Porter, Noah. *The New England Meeting House.* New Haven: Yale University Press, 1933.

Sinnott, Edmund W. *Meetinghouse & Church in Early New England.* New York: McGraw-Hill Book Co., 1963.

Speare, Eva A. *Colonial Meeting Houses of New Hampshire Compared with Their Contemporaries in New England.* Littleton, N. H.: Daughters of Colonial Wars, State of New. Hampshire, 1938.

Swartwout, Edgerton. *An Architectural Monograph: Some Old Time Churches of Vermont.* New York: R. F. Whitehead, c. 1927.

Wright, Charles A. *Some Old Time Meeting Houses of the Connecticut Valley.* Chicopee Falls, Mass.: Rich Print, 1911.

Methodist:

Clark, Elmer T. *An Album of Methodist History.* New York and Nashville: Abingdon-Cokesbury Press, 1952.

Division of National Missions of the Methodist Church. *Sanctuary Planning.* Philadelphia: Board of Missions, 1962.

Dolbey, George W. *The Architectural Expression of Methodism: The First Hundred Years.* London: Epworth Press, 1964.

Fudge, Alan G. *Church Design.* London: Epworth Press, 1950.

Jobson, F. J. *Chapel and School Architecture as Appropriate to the Buildings of Nonconformists, Particularly to Those of the Wesleyan Methodists with Practical Directions for the Erection of Chapels and School-Houses.* London: Hamilton, Adams, & Co., 1850.

Little, C. Deane. "Early Methodist Octagons," *Proceedings of the Wesley Historical Society,* XXV (1946), 81–6.

Perkins, E. Benson and Albert Hearn. *The Methodist Church Builds Again; A Consideration of the Purpose, Principles, and Plans for Methodist Church Building.* London: Epworth Press, 1946.

White, James F. "Early Methodist Liturgical Architecture," *Motive*, XVIII (1958), 12–13, 19–20.

—— *Notes on the Design of Methodist Student Centers.* Nashville: Methodist Student Movement, 1961.

Wilkins, John R. *Let's Build.* Revised edition; New York: Abingdon Press, 1961.

Others:

Faulkner, Charles D. *Christian Science Church Edifices.* 2nd edition; Chicago: C. D. Faulkner, 1946.

Hayes, John R. *Old Quaker Meeting-Houses.* 2nd edition; Philadelphia: Biddle Press, 1911.

Holt, Luther M. *Christian Science Church Architecture, Giving Exterior and Interior Views.* Los Angeles: Press of Times-Mirror Printing and Binding House, 1908.

Leavitt, Percy M. *Souvenir Portfolio of Universalist Churches in Massachusetts.* Boston: The Massasoit Press, 1906.

Richardson, Kenneth E. "A Guide for Planning Baptist Church Buildings," *American Institute of Architects Journal*, XXXVII (1962), 63–6.

Short, H. Lismer. "The Evolution of Unitarian Church Buildings," *Transactions of the Unitarian Historical Society* (1949), 146–53.

Index